Restoring t

Healing From Childhood Trauma

A Self-Help Journey to Overcoming the Pain and Abuse of Our Past

© 2025 by Melissa Alvis

All rights reserved.

No part of this book may be reproduced, stored in a retrieval system, or transmitted by any means – electronic, mechanical, photocopy, recording, or otherwise – without the prior permission of the copyright holder, except as provided by USA copyright law.

ISBN: 9798304891141 Paperback

ISBN: 9798304891424 Hardcover

Disclaimer

The information in this book, *Restoring the Broken Pieces: Healing from Childhood Trauma*, is only intended for educational and inspirational purposes. As a life coach, I aim to provide guidance, tools, and insights to support your healing journey, but I am not a licensed therapist, counselor, or medical professional. The concepts and techniques presented here are based on personal experiences, research, and coaching methodologies.

This book is not a substitute for professional therapy, medical advice, or diagnosis. If you are experiencing significant emotional distress, have a history of mental health concerns, or are in crisis, I strongly encourage you to seek the help of a qualified mental health professional or licensed therapist. Healing from childhood trauma can be a complex and deeply personal process, and professional support is often essential for navigating that journey safely and effectively.

While I strive to present accurate and reliable information, every person's experience is unique, and results may vary. Please use discretion and consult a qualified professional before implementing any strategies or practices discussed in this book. If at any point you feel overwhelmed or unsafe, reach out to a trusted professional or crisis hotline in your area.

By engaging with this material, you acknowledge that your healing journey is your responsibility and that the content of this book is intended to support, not replace professional care.

Thank you for allowing me to accompany you toward healing, growth, and restoration.

Dedication

*To my beloved sisters and brothers,
Bobbie Robin, Jana Kay, Wayne Lee, and Jimmy Joe,
who walked with me through our childhood trauma.
This book is for you – for your courage and resilience
despite the difficulties we faced.*

*To Dr. Neecie Moore,
My mentor and my guide,
whose wisdom and compassion illuminated
the path toward understanding and healing.
Your life coaching and unwavering support
have forever changed my life.*

Visit Our Website:

Hoping2Heal.com

"Turning Wounds into Wisdom One Day at a Time"

We invite you to explore **Hoping2Heal.com**, the companion website for Restoring the Broken Pieces.

You will find additional resources, journaling prompts, exercises, and encouragement to support your healing journey here. Connect with a community of like-minded individuals, access exclusive content, and stay updated on new tools and insights to help you turn your wounds into wisdom.

Thank you for allowing us to walk with you on this path to healing. Visit us at **Hoping2Heal.com** and take the next step toward restoration and renewal.

Contents

Dedication iii
Contents v
Preface vii
How to Use This Book xi
Introduction 1
Chapter 1: Understanding Childhood Trauma 5
Chapter 2: Trauma Lingers into Adulthood 21
Chapter 3: Discovering Our Inner Child 37
Chapter 4: Releasing the Pain of Our Past 53
Chapter 5: Managing Trauma Triggers 69
Chapter 6: The Power of Forgiveness 83
Chapter 7: Seeking Professional Support 97
Chapter 8: Writing Our New Narrative 111
Chapter 9: Sustaining Our Healing Journey 129
Chapter 10: Healing the Wounds of Complex Trauma 143
Conclusion 155
Appendix 159
Glossary of Terms 169
References 173
The Power of Reflection: Journal Prompts for Healing 177

Preface

My healing from childhood trauma has been a transformative process. What began as a desperate attempt to understand my pain has become a life of freedom, resilience, and hope. The weight of the past, marked by abuse and despair, once defined my world. But in seeking relief, I have understood that brokenness is where restoration begins. In this book, I offer lessons learned, tools, reflections, and a shared hope for all navigating their path to recovery and healing.

My journey began when I met Nadine, a petite, gentle lady who, at first glance, reminded me of my mom. She was the first person who helped me see the cycles of abuse for what they were: generational patterns that did not start with me but could end with me. Her wisdom gave me the courage to break those cycles. With only one bed left at her transitional house, Nadine took a lost, hurting, and "scared" young girl and gave her a chance at life. Thank you, Nadine, for being so dedicated to working with lost and hurting women. I will be forever indebted to you.

Alongside Nadine's counsel came a newfound faith. My conversion to Christianity brought clarity and strength, offering me the courage to move forward and begin life anew. Through God's Word, I found wisdom, guidance, and strength to rewrite my story.

Another cornerstone of healing for me has been my marriage. My husband and I have grown together, supporting one another as we've confronted our wounds and celebrated our victories. Our love has been a testament to the power of partnership and mutual respect. His encouragement inspired me to take several "first steps" towards personal growth and healing. What it resulted in was a greater understanding of my self-doubt, fears, and the emotional pain I had carried my entire life. I wanted to be free of the past and be my best self for God and my husband. Together, we've learned to transform our pain into purpose. Gregory, my dear husband, you have always been my cheerleader, a champion in your own right. I would not have accomplished all I did had it not been for your belief in me. Thank you for all of your support, encouragement, and tireless efforts in being my rock and my hero!

My healing journey would not have come to fruition without Dr. Neecie Moore and her life coach training, which provided a framework for much of what I had long felt but could not articulate. Through her teaching, I began to understand trauma, its effects, and the way it shapes our inner child. Her lessons on healing offered tools that illuminated the path forward, helping me identify and nurture the wounded parts of myself. Under her direction, I began to confront my past and embrace the idea that restoration was not just possible but necessary. Neecie, thank you for your tireless efforts to help others, as you also have been helped. My life has changed because of you. My heart, which was once held together with invisible, shameful threads, is now open and continues to experience healing each and every day.

This book is dedicated to my sisters and brothers, who lived through the turmoil in those early years alongside me. I felt deeply responsible for Robin but was never powerful enough to protect her. Jana Kay, my "twin," with whom I held a close-knit bond—probably because we were the opposite. Her strengths were my weaknesses, whereas her weaknesses were my strengths. We subconsciously depended on each other while caring for Mom and the boys. And to my beloved brothers, Wayne Lee, and Jimmy Joe, if there were anything I could change, it would have been to have stayed and taken care of you or brought you with me.

To Wendy, my Mom, I will never forget you as the beautiful lady you were. I loved how you laughed and sang. I loved when you would say, "I love you more than all the stars in the sky," and "I love you more than all of the grains of sand." We called each other "ladybug". You told me I could be anything I wanted to be. Mom, I knew early on that your life was not okay. It tore my heart apart to watch you live the way you did. But through it all, you tried to make our house a home. Mom, I will always love you!

Dear reader, as you embark on a journey with me through the pages of this book, thank you for your willingness to explore a new way of living. Healing from childhood trauma is not an easy road, but it is one worth taking. Together, we can search for a new life and narrative that moves beyond survival and into the fullness of freedom, joy, and peace. Let this book be a companion as you restore your broken pieces. We can do this together.

With compassion and hope,

Melissa Alvis

How to Use This Book

Thank you for choosing *Restoring the Broken Pieces: Healing from Childhood Trauma* as a companion on your healing journey. This book is more than just a guide; it bridges the transition between self-help and deeper therapeutic work. Whether you are navigating this path alone or working alongside a therapist, the tools and insights within these pages are designed to support, empower, and encourage you. Here is how to get the most out of this book:

1. Recognize This Book as a Bridge

This book complements your healing process, whether you start alone or in therapy. Use it to:

- Begin understanding the layers of trauma and how they affect your life.

- Prepare for or enhance therapeutic sessions with deeper insights into your experiences.

- Build a foundation of self-awareness and proactive healing strategies.

2. Embrace the Interactive Components

Healing is not passive—it is an active journey. Throughout this book, you'll find:

- Journal Prompts to help you explore your thoughts and emotions.

- Exercises that encourage self-reflection and growth.

- Worksheets to organize your insights and enhance your progress.

Take time to engage fully with these tools. The more effort you put in, the greater the rewards.

3. Create a Safe Space for Healing

Healing from trauma requires vulnerability and focus. To fully immerse yourself in this process:

- Find a quiet and safe environment where you can reflect without distractions.
- Establish a consistent routine for working through the book, whether daily, weekly, or at a pace that feels right for you.

4. Be Intentional and Proactive

Healing is not something that happens to you—it is something you create. Commit to:

- Showing up for yourself with honesty and determination.
- Setting realistic goals and holding yourself accountable.
- Taking breaks when needed but always returning to the work.

5. Incorporate Meditation and Reflection

To address the core issues of your pain and abuse, take time to:

- Meditate on the lessons and prompts within each chapter.
- Reflect deeply on your experiences, noticing patterns and triggers.
- Consider incorporating breathing exercises or utilizing mindfulness practices to stay grounded.

6. Connect with Your Past to Move Forward

Healing requires facing the difficult truths of your past. This book will gently guide you to:

- Acknowledge and process the pain of your experiences.
- Work through feelings of shame, guilt, and anger with compassion.
- Begin reframing your story to find resolution and empowerment.

7. Celebrate Small Wins

Every step in your recovery process is a victory. Remember to:

- Recognize the courage it takes to confront your trauma.
- Celebrate milestones, whether completing an exercise or having an emotional breakthrough.
- Reward yourself for your hard work, even in small ways, to reinforce your progress.

8. A Message of Gratitude

Thank you for trusting this book as part of your journey. Healing from childhood trauma is not easy, but your willingness to engage with this material shows incredible strength. May this book provide insight, comfort, and hope as you work to restore the broken pieces of your life. You are not alone, and every page reminds you of that. Together, let us begin the healing journey.

Introduction

Childhood trauma is something no one should have to experience, yet far too many of us carry the scars of pain and abuse into our adult lives. My husband and I are among those who endured childhood trauma, and it has only been through the care and concern of a beloved therapist, along with years of reflection and hard work, that we have come to a place where we can share our stories and help others begin their journey toward recovery.

This book, *Restoring the Broken Pieces: Healing from Childhood Trauma*, was born from our desire to reach those who are struggling to heal from the deep wounds of emotional, physical, or sexual abuse—victims who have not been able to connect with a counselor or therapist for any number of reasons. We were in that spot for many years, not knowing where or who to turn to. Thus, we know firsthand what it is like to feel suffocated by the past, haunted by triggers and memories that refuse to loosen their grip on our thoughts and feelings.

We have learned how much our childhood experiences shaped us in ways we only realized or understood later in life. Like many of you reading this book, we learned to cope, or a better word might be to survive. However, we did not begin the healing process until our lives crossed paths with someone who became my mentor as a life coach. She explained during many months of training that, the pain we experienced as children had followed us into adulthood, manifesting itself in our struggles with self-worth, in conflicted relationships, and in our ability to feel safe and at peace. Our healing journey has been long and, at times, arduous. However, it has also been transformative. We know that for us, a self-help book on healing from the pain and abuse of our past would have been a welcome addition to our home. We hope it will be for you as well.

This book is not just about understanding trauma; it is about finding ways to begin healing from it. I believe deeply in the power of reflection, journaling, and taking practical steps to create a solution. I incorporate tools in the book to help guide you as you take each step toward recovery. I hope these tools allow you to unpack the pain and abuse of your childhood, garner the courage to confront it, and ultimately lose its hold over your life.

In writing *Restoring the Broken Pieces: Healing from Childhood Trauma*, my husband and I decided to share our personal stories—our sometimes raw but honest truths about how trauma impacted us. We wrestled with this idea because we did not want our stories to become triggers for any of our readers. However, we think it is crucial to accompany you as a fellow traveler on this healing journey; thus, we will share some of our past.

From the outset, I want to explain who I have written this book for. *Restoring the Broken Pieces* is suited for adult survivors of childhood trauma who may not be ready to seek professional help but who want to understand what happened to them, how the effects linger on into adulthood, and what steps to take on their journey to overcome the pain and abuse of their past.

I write with a three-fold objective. First, I want to share what clinicians have taught us about the effects of childhood trauma. How do we define it, and to what extent does it impact us in adulthood? Secondly, I want to provide practical steps—tools, if you will—that have worked in our lives and the lives of fellow survivors we know. Finally, I want to encourage you to share your story in a community that understands, preferably with a community led by professionals who have spent their careers helping people like you and me. Sharing our story requires a ton of courage due to the need to develop trust in others, and this has always been the most challenging part of recovery for me, but it has provided the most rewarding moments of my healing journey as well.

Whether you have just started your journey or have been on this path for a while, I hope this book provides the support you need in this season of your life—that *Restoring the Broken Pieces* helps you reframe the past, rediscover your true self, and find peace and resilience for a brighter future. This book is more than a roadmap to healing from childhood trauma. It is an opportunity to rebuild your life and create a new lifelong narrative for yourself. A narrative not defined by the pain and abuse of your past but by the growth and beauty you discover along your journey of healing.

It is an honor to come alongside you during this time. Are you ready to restore the broken pieces of your past? Then let us get busy. Please know that I am here to help.

Chapter 1
Understanding Childhood Trauma

Tucked away in one of our closets are boxes of sports memorabilia my husband has held onto for decades. He grew up a fan of all sports, but in particular, a baseball guy. His favorite team growing up was the St. Louis Cardinals. That's because his grandfather was a big Cardinals fan. What I did not know about those early days or any of the memories attached to the memorabilia he still has was the importance of a particular book held in his past.

My husband was raised without his biological dad, who was serving in the United States Army during those early years, stationed in Germany. His mom was employed full-time, so most of his days and nights were spent at his grandparents' (Nanny & Pa) house. There, he became attached to Pa, his constant companion, best friend, and father figure. There was a problem, however. Pa was an alcoholic and a child molester, so my husband was constantly bombarded with sexual abuse early on. From the age of four, at least, that is about how far back he can remember, until the age of seven, when the family moved to a town sixty miles away, my husband was victimized. The irony is that the only person he bonded with as a small child was the person he was most afraid of during those early years. To this day, he can recall many nights when he and Pa were nestled in a La-Z-Boy chair, Nanny was asleep in another room, and Pa was doing things that created confusion and fear in my husband. He would eventually put up a fight, wiggle out of the grasp of his Pa, and run over to an area of the living room he felt safe in. He would always grab the same baseball book and sit there, trying to ignore Pa's coaxing. To this day, my husband would tell you that the sight of that baseball almanac still brings mixed emotions.

In this chapter, we will define childhood trauma, describe its impact on children over time, and discuss the Neuroscience underlying it. Trauma is not just some random event that has happened in our past. It feels more like a wound we do not know is even there. It has this subtle yet powerful influence on how we develop as children and, just as importantly, how we think, feel, and interact with others as adults. Trauma left unresolved removes our ability to discover our true selves.

Defining Childhood Trauma

Childhood trauma refers to experiences in a child's life that can impair their ability to cope with situations and process their emotions, leaving psychological, emotional, and even physical scars that persist into adulthood (Van der Kolk, 2014). Unlike the ordinary stressors a child might face in their day-to-day activities, trauma can disrupt their sense of stability and safety.

So, what is a traumatic event? According to the American Psychological Association website (https://www.apa.org), a traumatic event is a frightening, dangerous, or violent event that poses bodily harm or a threat to a child's life or a loved one. Another name for such events that is used descriptively is Adverse Childhood Experiences (ACEs). These are traumatic events that happen to children from the time of birth until the age of 17. They can lead to lifelong health complications, which may include mental health conditions, chronic physical maladies, and substance use.

The Center for Disease Control (CDC) and medical giant Kaiser Permanente ran a study from 1995-1997 on the effects of child abuse and neglect (Felitti et al., 1998). The study found ten different types of traumas that typically impact most victims. They coined Adverse Childhood Experiences (ACE) to describe these occurrences. The 10 ACEs of trauma, according to their study outcomes, are:

- Physical Abuse
- Emotional Abuse
- Sexual Abuse
- Physical Neglect
- Emotional Neglect
- Mental Illness in a family member
- Divorce of parents
- Substance abuse in their environment
- Domestic Violence
- Having a loved one incarcerated

There are additional concepts we can place alongside that list, including bullying, living in a war-torn area, acts of terrorism, shootings, accidents, and natural disasters. It is estimated that 60%–80% of adults in the United States have experienced at least one type of ACE. Many of us experienced multiple ACEs in our childhood. This is unsettling to me due to the number of ACEs I have been exposed to. What about you? How many of these events define your childhood?

Trauma's Impact Over Time

I wondered for many years what was wrong with me. I tended to internalize fear much more than others. I avoided situations and events that reminded me of past negative experiences. I would be indecisive and lean on others for direction when it was not necessary. Then, I discovered what the signs of an adverse childhood experience were. It read like the story of my life as a young adult. The list of outcomes found in the CDC Kaiser Permanente study included:

- Traumatic Brain Injury
- Depression, Anxiety, Suicide
- Post-Traumatic Stress Disorder
- Phobias
- Mood and eating disorders
- Unintended Pregnancy
- Substance Use
- Lower Educational, Occupational, and Income levels

This was a lightbulb moment in my life. I realized there were underlying causes for the struggles I was enduring, and more importantly, they were the result of things done to me—not things I had planned for and created myself. My perspective changed, as I understood for the first time that I was not to blame. As you look at your past, can you see the same scenario in your life? Do you understand you are not at fault for what others have done to you?

Understanding the Underlying Neuroscience

Neuroscience is the scientific study of the nervous system, including the brain, the spinal cord, and the peripheral nervous system. Taking a brief look at the science behind childhood trauma will help explain what is happening to us because of the abuse we have incurred in the past. When trauma occurs in our childhood, brain scans show a marked difference in brain development, affecting neural pathways and causing symptoms of chronic stress like physical Illness, hormonal imbalances, and mental health problems, including anxiety, depression, and PTSD (Lippard, E. T. C., & Nemeroff, C. B., 2019).

The triune brain model developed by neuroscientist Paul D. MacLean (MacLean et al., 1990) further explains what is going on when we are exposed to childhood trauma. His theory holds that the brain is divided into three parts, from simple to complex. They are:

- **Reptilian Brain:** This part of our brain manages autonomic body processes like breathing, hunger, and thirst. It is also where our survival instincts are located.

- **Mammalian Brain:** This part of the brain manages the limbic system, which regulates our emotions and attachment styles.

- **Neomammalian Brain:** This part of our brain manages learning, memory, decision-making, sensory processing, and complex problem-solving.

When we experience trauma, the brain shuts down all non-essential activities and moves us into the lower brain systems. This movement activates the sympathetic nervous system and signals the release of stress hormones, preparing us for survival mode: fight-or-flight-or-freeze-or-fawn responses to the trauma-induced event. Once the trauma event has passed, the parasympathetic nervous system returns, allowing our brain to resume regular activity with all three parts. As you can imagine, a single event would likely allow a quicker return to normalcy of brain activity. Whereas a chronic pattern of trauma, which many of us have experienced, increases the difficulty of returning to normal brain functions. We are constantly stressed and unable to relax and be normal children.

Here are the brain's reactions to what could be considered fearful situations or extended periods of adverse childhood experiences (ACEs). Which response do you see in yourself?

- The **Fight** response is exhibited through a temper outburst that may be unpredictable and even explosive. This is the aggressive yell or scream, the slamming of doors, and always feeling threatened. So, protection at all costs is the mantra.

- The **Flight** response feels easily trapped by its situation. This response style has a history of abruptly ending relationships out of fear, rushing around, and avoiding any downtime for reflection.

- The **Freeze** response shuts down with complete avoidance. This style struggles with what is real or unreal. There is a tendency to hide out, procrastinate, and often give up.

- The **Fawn** response, which I have experienced the most in my life, is associated with being a people-pleaser, having a fear of saying 'no,' being overly polite and agreeable, and unduly reliant on others to help solve problems.

While traumatic events can harm us at any age, the trauma we experience as children is much more severe. During those early years, our brains are still developing. Specifically, adverse childhood experiences target our hippocampus (memory), areas of the brain that help us think logically (prefrontal cortex), and our amygdala (where we process emotions). All of this can be overwhelming when we first understand it. However, there is hope. As we will discover in a later chapter, rewiring the brain is possible. The term used for such work is *Neuroplasticity*. I know it can happen due to my life experience and because I have witnessed it in the lives of others in my circle of influence. It can happen to you, too.

The Importance of Attachment Styles

Another area that impacts us through childhood trauma is our attachment style in relationships. John Bowlby founded attachment style theory in the 1950s (Bowlby, J., 1969), and Mary Ainsworth (Ainsworth et al., 1978) later expanded upon it. Attachment theory outlines how our primary caregivers bonded with us, which sets the foundation for how we will navigate relationships throughout our lives. The research by Ainsworth categorized four different types of attachment styles. They are:

- **Secure:** This style can regulate emotions, easily trust others, have practical communication skills, be comfortable in relationships, manage conflict well, and seek emotional support.
- **Avoidant:** This style avoids emotional or physical intimacy, is independent, is uncomfortable expressing feelings, is dismissive of others, and feels threatened easily.

- **Anxious:** This style has low self-esteem, feels unworthy of love, needs approval from others, is highly sensitive to criticism, and has a significant fear of abandonment.

- **Disorganized:** This style fears rejection, has high levels of anxiety, has difficulty trusting others, and exhibits signs of both the avoidant and anxious attachment styles.

Before closing this chapter, I want to touch on another measurement of childhood trauma. These would be the categories of childhood trauma. Clinicians classify trauma in one of the following ways:

- **Acute Trauma:** This refers to a single event that is more than what the child can cope with. Examples would include accidents, witnessing violence, or a natural disaster.

- **Chronic Trauma:** This would result from prolonged exposure to harmful events. Examples would include domestic violence and repeated physical, emotional, or sexual abuse. These would be areas that disrupt the development of a child.

- **Complex Trauma:** This would result from a child being exposed to multiple forms of abuse, profoundly impacting the child's emotional state, development, and safety.

In conclusion, our understanding of childhood trauma is the foundation for moving forward. We have seen how impactful trauma can be, and we have lived lives that validate that idea. As adult survivors, our goals must include looking at our past, acknowledging the pain, comforting the inner child, reframing our self-perception and self-esteem, and creating a course of correction that provides a voice to our present state and hope for our future. We were not designed to be victims. We were intended to be gifts to the world around us. I look forward to our healing journey together. We now need to look at how trauma lingers into adulthood.

Key Takeaways

- Trauma left unresolved removes our ability to discover our true selves.

- Unlike ordinary stressors in a child's day-to-day life, trauma disrupts their sense of stability and safety.

- The list of outcomes from childhood trauma can include brain injury, depression, anxiety, PTSD, phobias, and substance use.

- Brain scans exhibit a marked difference for those impacted by childhood trauma.

- The results of a traumatic event in the life of a child include the release of stress hormones, which prepare us for the fight-or-flight-or-freeze-or-fawn responses.

- Childhood trauma targets our hippocampus (memory), areas of the brain that help us think logically (prefrontal cortex), and our amygdala (where we process our emotions).

- Attachment theory outlines how our primary caregivers bonded with us.

Chapter 1 Journal

1. If you could go back in time, what would be the one thing you would most want to change about your childhood?

_____

Chapter 1 Journal

2. What will be most challenging to discuss during your healing journey?

Chapter 1 Journal

3. Were there times in your childhood when you internalized feelings of shame or guilt? Do you think this shaped the way you view yourself today?

Chapter 1 Journal

4. One of my favorite songs is entitled "Dear Younger Me", which is about being able to talk to our younger self. If you could do that, what would you say to yourself?

_____
_____
_____
_____
_____
_____
_____
_____
_____
_____
_____
_____
_____
_____
_____
_____
_____
_____
_____
_____
_____
_____

Chapter 1 Exercise

When my husband was working through his childhood trauma, he decided to create what he called "A Life Map." He drew every year he could remember on paper with the corresponding months. He then attached his memories to the correct date on the map. It looked like this:

1978

Jan	**Feb**	**Mar**	**April**	**May**	**June**
Event		Event		Event	

July	**Aug**	**Sep**	**Oct**	**Nov**	**Dec**
Event		Event		Event	

Under each of the months, he would place events that were attached to what he believed were trauma. It helped him to recall what was in his subconscious memory. Maybe you could do the same. You can call it your trauma timeline.

Chapter 1 Worksheet

One of the hardest things to do is to recall those memories of pain and abuse. It is difficult for those just starting their healing journey, much less to talk about. On the worksheet below, identify the areas of trauma you have been exposed to. If you can, write how that impacted you.

ACE Event	Your Reflection on the Event
Physical Abuse	
Emotional Abuse	
Sexual Abuse	
Physical Neglect	
Emotional Neglect	
Mental Illness in Family	
Parents' Divorce	
Substance Use in the Home	
Domestic Violence	
Loved One Incarcerated	
Bullying	
Other	

Chapter 2
Trauma Lingers into Adulthood

I was an innocent eight-year-old child the day my mom married my stepfather. What should have been a joyous occasion for me and my siblings turned into a moment of life-changing grief when I was introduced to childhood trauma. I will never forget the moment my stepfather took me into the bathroom on his wedding night and made me take my clothes off. This began a decade-long exposure to episodes we learned in Chapter 1 as adverse childhood experiences. This would include being molested by my mom's father at the age of ten, watching years of domestic violence being committed by my stepfather, and being raped by a boyfriend at the age of sixteen.

One of the most challenging aspects of being a survivor of childhood trauma is looking back and seeing when and how we became objects of other people's wrongful intent. For me, this is especially painful due to my reaching out to my mom during the early years of my abuse only to be told, "We do not talk about those things." This was when I learned I did not have a voice. I knew that whatever happened to me was the way things were. Looking back, I see that the silence in me being validated in multiple ways was more disturbing. I can remember the police being called to our house for domestic violence. As they left our home, they responded that this was "a domestic dispute." My stepfather was never held accountable. And after he hit me, I began forming a connection that love was somehow equated with abuse. He would hit us and then say he was sorry and loved us. So, my understanding of love was to link abuse with relationships. This idea would permeate my life for years as an adult.

In this chapter, we are going to look at how those lingering effects of trauma have followed us into adulthood. We are going to examine how unresolved trauma influences adult relationships, our emotional development, and our self-worth. We do not realize that our behavior is often a result of the past. However, we usually make decisions based on the pain and abuse that are derived from our adverse childhood experiences.

Childhood trauma can also induce Post-Traumatic Stress Disorder (PTSD), which can lead into adulthood and impact not only our mental health but also our daily lives. Trauma experienced in our formative years can cause the brain to remain in a heightened state of alert, looking for potential threats. This hyper-vigilance is our brain's way of preventing harm, even when no danger exists (Van der Kolk, 2014). Moreover, this hyper-vigilance can result from any of the adverse childhood experiences, including neglect.

Lingering Effects of Childhood Trauma

What has always been a psychological struggle for me is the distressing nature of flashbacks. For many years as an adult, I experienced triggers that seemingly appeared out of nowhere. I have read that these triggers were rooted in memories yet to be processed. This was true for my husband as well. He went from adolescence into adulthood without remembering parts of his past. As he began examining his adverse childhood experiences, he started recalling events he had long repressed in his subconscious. Studies indicate that Complex PTSD can lead to actual structural changes in the hippocampus and amygdala, which are associated with memory and emotional responses (Briere & Scott, 2015). As survivors, we can take solace in the fact that any symptoms we see and experience are involuntary and not a result of some failure on our part.

Another area I have struggled with since childhood is what I would call an emotional numbing of my feelings. This led me to experience depression and anxiety at times in my life. The idea of being a victim and not having a voice contributed significantly to a sense of unworthiness and hopelessness. It was like a cycle of psychological turmoil that would occur every so often. I would feel a lack of self-worth and self-esteem and work diligently to remind myself of my value to my husband, siblings, and friends, only to see short-term results of feeling good about my life. Triggers would then raise doubts again, and I would be in the same cycle of devaluing my worth and the world around me. The previously mentioned fawn response by me to apparent threats would reinforce my need to be a people pleaser, unable to say no, and becoming overly reliant on others for decisions that should have been easy for me to make.

The Impact of Trauma on Emotional Development and Self-Worth

A constant exposure to such ideas about my value, or lack thereof, led to additional bouts of depression and anxiety. This was due to the self-blame I took from my adverse childhood experiences. When my stepfather was committing domestic violence toward our family, he was always remorseful afterward, with his typical "I am sorry verbiage." Therefore, as a child, I began forming a connection between love and abuse, thinking I was somehow responsible for his behavior. I was the one to blame, which created additional cycles of fault-finding where I thought my weakness or my inadequacies were the source of the abuse I was experiencing. I guess it was my way of rationalizing the patterns of abuse I was seeing in my life as a child. I am not sure. I am sure this type of thinking led to shame and guilt that has taken decades to understand and resolve.

The Impact of Trauma on Relationships

The outcome of a troubled childhood had a significant impact on my ability to form relationships once into adolescence and adulthood. How could I form bonds with others and develop trust in relationships when I had learned not to trust those closest to me? One study has indicated that the fear of emotional intimacy stems from a learned association between closeness and potential harm. This is rooted in betrayal by caregivers early in life. In adulthood, this fear can leave survivors struggling to engage in relationships or feel connected, even when they develop a level of trust (Liotti & Farina, 2016).

In Chapter 1, we looked briefly at the attachment styles we develop as children based primarily on how our caregivers bond with us. This plays a significant role in how we interact with others in adulthood. The style I consistently held to was the disorganized attachment. With it, I would create an unpredictable relationship pattern, sometimes seeking closeness and only reacting fearfully once engaged in a relationship. I was trying to understand the risks versus rewards of healthy relationships. Ones that had boundaries and were rooted in understanding my self-compassion and self-care. I wish I had learned how to communicate more openly about attachment issues earlier in my life. It would have provided me with healthier and more fulfilling relationships as an adult.

The Influence of Triggers

As I write this book, emotional triggers tied to memories I thought were resolved have returned to the surface. Years ago, those same triggers felt like landmines for me emotionally. It has taken decades of practicing mindfulness techniques and acknowledging the presence of those emotional landmines in my past to produce greater levels of resiliency and stability in my life. Emotional triggers are a significant challenge we must be prepared to face head-on in our healing journey.

You may be wondering how my husband and I got through those early years of adulthood and have accumulated over thirty-five years of marriage. I was an expert at putting up emotional walls as a form of self-protection. For his part, my husband struggled early on in our marriage with trust issues. He, too, put up emotional walls. So, how did we make it through the challenges we faced relationally? We would say, "one day at a time." In all honesty, it has taken hard work and practice. It has required that I spend more time investing in him; he is doing the same for me daily. This has been our way of supporting each other's healing journey. It is also why I will dedicate pages later in the book to the importance of finding support groups to assist in your healing journey. Our relationships become powerful avenues for mutual growth and support when needed.

The Effects of Defense Mechanisms

There are additional aspects concerning the lingering effects of our childhood trauma that persist into adulthood. These are defense mechanisms. Although they have often been a way for my husband and me to protect ourselves emotionally from the pain of our past, we have discovered that the long-term effects may have been counterproductive to our healing journey. If we were to relive those years, I am sure we would use these same tools to shield us from the full impact of our trauma experiences. However, we must admit that they hindered our ability to heal quickly and live more authentically. Some of the tools, coping mechanisms if you will, we used include the following:

- **Avoidance:** Although this behavior seemed protective early on, it never allowed us to move past the reality of our pain. We discovered that limiting our exposure to childhood stories increased our fear of the past. We had to find a purpose for the pain, and that meant opening up to each other about the things that we had kept hidden for so long.

- **Dissociation:** This was our default coping mechanism early in life because this became our way of "checking out." We did everything in our adolescence and early adulthood to escape those overwhelming memories and the emotions they produced.

- **Emotional Suppression:** We attempted to remain in survival mode by not facing our underlying issues of fear, anger, and/or sadness. But those emotions never went away and could not be processed in an emotionally healthy way until we became proactive about talking through them with one another.

The Stages of Grief

One of the breakthrough moments of our healing journey was when my husband volunteered for a hospice care program. While being trained, he was introduced to the work of Dr. Elizabeth Kubler-Ross, a pioneer in near-death studies. In her book "On Death and Dying" (Kübler-Ross, E., 1969), she discusses her theory on the stages of grief. Our learning about these stages helped us immensely as we processed the pain of our past. We were able to look at our grieving process as we recalled the pain of our childhood trauma.

Dr. Kubler-Ross believed that those who were experiencing grief would go through a series of five emotional stages in processing their pain. These stages included the following:

- **Shock and Denial:** In this first stage, we cry, "No, this cannot happen!" We are not equipped to process all the emotions involved, so denial acts like a buffer, helping us to face those feelings at a pace we can handle.

- **Rage and Anger:** In this stage, we ask, "Why is this happening to me?" We question everything and everyone.

- **Bargaining:** This stage is filled with statements like, "What if..." or "If only..." During this stage, we attempt to arrive at a truce with the situation or with a higher power.

- **Depression:** In this stage, we acknowledge our reality, "Yes, it is me!" This often leads to profound grief, which can take us through levels of despair, resulting in depression.

- **Acceptance:** Here, we begin to accept the present circumstances and start living with a new perspective or a new normal.

The time we spent processing our grief as we looked at the past was significantly enhanced by understanding that what we were feeling was normal and to be expected in our recovery. We are so grateful for being taught those stages of grief.

My takeaway is that the lingering effects of childhood trauma have been a persistent theme in both my life as well as my husband's throughout our life together. The impact has been far-reaching, touching our emotional, psychological, and relational well-being. We have learned that the trauma we experienced as children has not only left a lasting imprint on our developing brain but also shaped our emotional responses and patterns of behavior as adults. In early adulthood, we struggled with anxiety and depression, we experienced difficulties with trust and self-worth, and we had to overcome those coping mechanisms that were deeply ingrained in our lives.

The impact of trauma on our relationship with one another as well as those in our circle of influence, whether that was family, co-workers, or those we were involved with in ministry or friendships, was profound at times. It was initially hard for us to form healthy attachments in relationships, mainly due to the fear of abandonment that was always at the core of our belief systems. However, we understand that those relationships are fundamentally meaningful for our lives. Moreover, we see first-hand how our practice of self-care and the cultivation of mindfulness techniques in our lives, individually and as a couple, have enabled us to grow significantly beyond the scars of childhood trauma. You, too, can do the same. The scars may never disappear, but with consistent effort and hard work, you can begin embracing your strengths, building healthy relationships, and finding hope and resilience on your healing journey. This begins with a look at our inner child.

Key Takeaways

- A potential problem for those affected by childhood trauma is the existence of flashbacks.

- Triggers are tied to emotional memories in our childhood.

- Triggers can lead to a constant sense of numbed feelings.

- Self-blame that results from childhood trauma can lead to bouts of anxiety and depression.

- The fear of intimacy in adulthood can stem from a learned association between closeness and potential harm. Betrayal in childhood by caregivers is the cause.

- One of the long-term effects of using defense mechanisms is that they can be counter-productive to long-term healing.

- Stages in the grieving process not only enlighten what we are experiencing as we are impacted by trauma but also remind us that the feelings we have are normal.

Chapter 2 Journal

1. Think about the times in your life, especially lately, when an emotional reaction has been strong when you have experienced fear, sadness, anger, or anxiety. How do you think these might be connected to your childhood?

_____
_____
_____
_____
_____
_____
_____
_____
_____
_____
_____
_____
_____
_____
_____
_____
_____
_____

Chapter 2 Journal

2. Consider how your past has shaped your sense of self-worth. What beliefs about yourself would you like to change?

_____
_____
_____
_____
_____
_____
_____
_____
_____
_____
_____
_____
_____
_____
_____
_____
_____
_____
_____
_____
_____
_____
_____

Chapter 2 Journal

3. Has it been hard for you to develop relationships? Are you like us when it comes to trusting others? In essence, is it hard to trust?

_____
_____
_____
_____
_____
_____
_____
_____
_____
_____
_____
_____
_____
_____
_____
_____
_____
_____
_____
_____

Chapter 2 Journal

4. How do emotional triggers affect your day-to-day living right now? Do these triggers cause you stress, make you feel like disconnecting, or lead you into coping mechanisms?

_____
_____
_____
_____
_____
_____
_____
_____
_____
_____
_____
_____
_____
_____
_____
_____
_____
_____
_____
_____
_____
_____
_____
_____

Chapter 2 Exercise

Imagine you have a friend who has gone through similar circumstances as you in their childhood. You know they are struggling right now with triggers and the resulting emotions. Can you write them a letter of encouragement? And can you reflect on what you would say if that friend were you?

_____
_____
_____
_____
_____
_____
_____
_____
_____
_____
_____
_____
_____
_____
_____
_____
_____
_____
_____

RESTORING THE BROKEN PIECES

Chapter 2 Worksheet

This activity is designed to help you understand how childhood trauma may affect you in adulthood.

- Consider a recent event when you felt a strong emotion like anger, anxiety, or fear. Briefly describe what happened. Is this a recurring theme in your life?

- Remind yourself that you matter. Tell yourself you are worthy of love and respect and can achieve whatever you desire. Write this down and place it everywhere in your home.

- Identify a current relationship challenge you are facing. Why do you think it is a struggle?

- Do you have a couple of ideas about how you can begin to implement change in your life right now?

Chapter 3
Discovering Our Inner Child

My husband was nine years old when his mom remarried. She married a man who was a greenskeeper on a golf course in the town they lived in. That first summer, he took my husband to work with him to ensure he was cared for. My husband would spend 8-10 hours daily trying to entertain himself and stay out of trouble.

There were times when his stepfather would take my husband through the back door of the country club. Each time they entered the building's kitchen area, they were met by a mentally challenged man who operated the dishwasher. My husband remembers vividly the man's stare as he watched this nine-year-old boy pass by.

One day, as my husband walked around the clubhouse, this dishwasher man motioned to help him get some canned goods from a cellar out back. My husband went down with the man and was coaxed to sit with him briefly. Before he realized it, the man tried to take my husband's clothes off. The man would not relinquish his grip until my husband began yelling. Once freed, my husband ran up the stairs and onto the grounds surrounding the clubhouse.

Looking back, my husband came to the realization of the effects this event generated. The fear that was produced stayed with my husband for the next few years because he continued to join his stepfather at work each summer. It was a fear much like the one he had faced with his Pa at an early age. A fear so overwhelming that he would not go back into the kitchen area. He also internalized a deep sense of shame. It was not his fault, but he experienced guilt and shame nonetheless. The shame was powerful enough to keep my husband from telling his stepfather what had happened. The trauma-based fear also produced an anger that my husband had experienced a few years before. Let me explain.

When my husband's family moved away from his grandfather Pa into a new town sixty miles away, the abuse ceased. But the results of the abuse did not. It would be less than a year before his mom would get a divorce from his biological dad. His dad had been home from the Army only a couple of years at the time of the divorce and was an angry man. He never hit my husband, and he does not remember his mom ever being struck. But the shouting, the slamming of doors, and angry words were deafening for my husband as a youth.

Just before his parents' divorce, they bought my husband a new bed, a small twin with a foam and vinyl headboard. At one point before the divorce, my husband took a pencil and began puncturing holes in the headboard—dozens and dozens of holes. Looking back, he cannot remember the event that provoked this rage. He remembers feeling afraid and emotionally distraught, though.

Two years after the destruction of the headboard, my husband acted out again. He recalls dozens of stray and feral cats residing in the bushes surrounding the golf course clubhouse. He would see these cats while standing safely above on the back patio. When the cats noticed him, they would hiss or snarl. In response, my husband began trying to locate rocks he could drop on the cats before they realized he was there. His fear of the dishwasher man was resonating now as anger. He wanted the cats to hurt, too. This incident with the cats directly resulted from the trauma my husband experienced with the dishwasher man. It was a manifestation of his unresolved anger and fear.

The title of this chapter is "Discovering Our Inner Child." My goals with this topic are to define the inner child, elaborate on why this topic matters to us, who are the survivors of childhood trauma, and discuss the wounds of our inner child. We will then examine the inner child's impact on our emotional development, identity, and self-worth. We will also touch on reconnecting with our inner child and show how we can provide healing to our younger selves. Here, I must emphasize the crucial role of professional care in this journey. Even though we will discuss therapeutic modalities for the healing process, the memories we have bound up in our childhood trauma need to be brought to the surface, and this is best done in a therapeutic environment with a trusted counselor.

Defining the Inner Child

So, what do I mean when I say inner child? The "inner child" is a psychological concept that reflects the childlike aspects of our personality that continue to exist within us, regardless of age. This part of us holds our formative years' emotions, memories, and innocence. Often, it is through our inner child that we connect with unprocessed emotions, unmet needs, and experiences that were not adequately addressed or nurtured in childhood. It represents our vulnerabilities and capacity for wonder, creativity, and joy. But it also embodies our resilience, healing ability, and growth potential.

I was first introduced to the inner child concept during a life coach certification program. The therapist, whom I consider my mentor, shared the teaching and vision of psychologist John Bradshaw. Mr. Bradshaw pioneered this field of study, and we should look at the foundational framework on which he based his work.

To grasp the inner child concept, Mr. Bradshaw would refer to Psychoanalyst Erik Erikson's stages of psychosocial development

(Erikson, E. H.,1950). Erikson's model outlines the various psychosocial crises individuals face at different stages of life. If these crises are not successfully resolved, a part of the individual remains fixated at that stage, continuing to affect them into adulthood. This, too, was highly frightening for me to read through the first time. The reason was that I felt a deficit in nearly every age group I could remember. My husband thought the same when reading the material the first time. Here are Erikson's first five stages of development:

- **Trust vs. Mistrust (Infancy):** If an infant experiences mistrust, they may find it difficult to trust others, affecting relationships and social interactions.

- **Autonomy vs. Shame and Doubt (Early Childhood):** Failure to develop a sense of independence can lead to feelings of shame and doubt, shattering confidence and interrupting the development of an independent spirit.

- **Initiative vs. Guilt (Preschool Age):** Struggles in this stage may result in a lack of initiative and an overbearing sense of guilt, which can affect ambition and creativity.

- **Industry vs. Inferiority (School Age):** If not resolved, this can lead to feelings of inferiority and a lack of confidence in abilities, which can influence academic and professional achievements.

- **Identity vs. Role Confusion (Adolescence):** Unresolved identity crises can lead to confusion about one's role in life, affecting career choices and personal relationships.

Why Understanding the Inner Child Matters

As you can see, the inner child impacts our adult lives in ways we may not always recognize. When our inner child's wounds go unaddressed, they can manifest in behaviors, relationships, and emotional patterns that seem out of alignment with our adult lives. The emotional triggers we experience—intense fears, feelings of abandonment, or unexplainable sadness—often signal unresolved pain from our childhood. I have noticed that repetitive behavior results from my wounded inner child. If I am in the workplace and someone asks a question, this means they do not have the answer. However, when I respond with an explanation and know it is correct, a mere questionable look on their part or a word of questioning sends me into no-confidence overdrive. My husband would tell you he is the same way. He would say he has seen deficits in every stage throughout his life.

I mentioned in the previous chapter that defense mechanisms can be seen in how we protect ourselves as children and develop into adolescence and adulthood. These become our coping strategies when we are overwhelmed by our emotions or environments. The long-term problem with these strategies is that they hinder our growth and prevent authentic relationships and a sense of self-worth. By defense mechanisms, I am referring, among others, to:

- **Repression:** This is the unconscious suppression of painful memories. My husband experienced this. He blotted out memories of abuse for many years into adulthood due to the immense pain they created.

- **Denial:** Children can refuse to accept the pain of their reality, especially in unsafe environments. Convincing themselves that all is right avoids dealing with the pain.

- **Regression:** Children can revert to earlier life developmental behaviors that provide a way to cope. An example would be my husband sucking his thumb up until the age of seven, which offered him a sense of comfort. Doing so allowed him to return to a behavior he associated with a safer time.

- **Fantasy and Imagination:** Children often retreat to a "make-believe" environment to avoid the pain of reality. While offering temporary relief, this pattern of behavior can distort coping skills as they develop.

- **Rationalization:** I have practiced this defense mechanism for a long time. This mechanism allowed me to make excuses for my caregiver's neglectful and abusive behavior and attribute their failings to me rather than them.

The Impact on Our Development

There are other defense mechanisms mentioned earlier that we exhibited as children in response to the trauma we experienced, and the long-term results of utilizing these survival tools shaped how we developed as children. The wounds of my inner child led to my carrying around feelings of inadequacy and worthlessness for many years. My husband would echo the same sentiment. He would say those feelings of inadequacy interfered with his self-confidence and self-worth for years into adulthood.

So, how do we connect with our inner child? Once again, I recommend you contact an experienced therapist who can provide a safe environment. This creates the level of trust needed for opening up those memories of pain and abuse. Until that time arrives, we can take several steps on this healing journey.

Reconnecting Leads to Healing

We can begin by recalling the happiest memories of our childhood. We can always imagine one we would have wanted to experience if none existed. What would you like to do as a child that never came to fruition? Grab your inner child by the hand and go there together. Remember that our inner child feels safer when we acknowledge them, remind them you are looking out for them, and voice your love for them. For me, my inner child would have difficulty trusting anyone because I did not have trust in the caregivers of my life as a child. I also had feelings of inferiority growing up and suppressed my emotions. These behavior patterns resulted from numerous unresolved issues I experienced as a child.

Next, there are several positive things I have learned to do for my inner child. No matter what point in my past I have sought to meet with the inner child in me, I have always striven to create a sense of trust and affirmation. I have always wanted to hug my inner child and remind them of their value and worth during that stage of my life. In the early years of my healing journey, I would write positive affirmations about myself and my life on sticky notes and place these everywhere in my home. I still practice this and have sticky notes from myself and my husband in various places of my house and workplace.

Another area of focus that has worked in my life over the years is practicing self-compassion. This has been exhibited chiefly through journaling. I have many notebooks and writing journals that have positivity as their theme. This is where I write extensively on the power of kindness toward myself. Journaling can also be a powerful tool for conversing with our inner child. Have you ever considered writing a letter to your inner child about what they experienced earlier in your life? I have discovered that this tool effectively reaches out to the hurting and wounded child of my past. It feels safer than trying to open up alone. It provides trust and allows me to experience my inner child on my terms.

One of the most challenging aspects of reaching out to our inner child is that there may be many stages of our early life that need to be touched upon. For my husband and me, there were various age levels at which we could remember trauma. To find peace, we had to reach out to our inner child at each age where the pain and abuse stemmed from. There is an increased difficulty in healing from trauma when there are numerous inner child wounds at different stages of our development.

In summation, doing inner child work is best done in a therapeutic environment—one which an experienced and trusted counselor leads. The goals of a self-help program are to create a safe place to visualize and connect with your inner child, bring comfort to the child you are connecting with, provide positive emotions to replace the underlying negative feelings of the past, and do this for each of the various stages of trauma that were experienced. Many tears may be shed in light of the pain stored up, but there is a reason to hope. Hope reminds us that while doing inner child work, we are more than reaching back to the pain and abuse of our past. We are also taking steps toward a future of growth and healing. The pathway to our inner child is not easy, yet it provides the avenue to accepting our past and creating an environment of self-love that has long been needed in our lives. Healing our inner child is an investment in our past and our future. Every moment we spend nurturing our inner child brings us closer to the person we were designed to be. And it allows us to begin embracing who we are. Let's now focus on releasing the pain of our past.

Key Takeaways

- Childhood memories brought to the surface in a therapeutic environment are key to healing.

- The inner child holds our formative year's emotions and memories.

- The inner child represents our vulnerabilities.

- The inner child embodies our resilience, healing ability, and growth potential.

- When our inner child wounds are not addressed, they can result in behaviors, relationships, and emotional patterns that are out of alignment with our adult lives.

- Defense mechanisms become our coping strategies when we are overwhelmed by our emotions or environments.

- Positive affirmations are key to creating a sense of trust in our inner child.

- When inner child wounds exist at different stages of our development, the effect increases difficulty during the healing process.

Chapter 3 Journal

1. Describe a time when you felt joy as a child. How might you connect with that feeling today?

Chapter 3 Journal

2. What does a "safe space" mean to you right now? How can you create such a place, so your inner child feels safe?

Chapter 3 Journal

3. Write a letter to your inner child. Please consider what words of encouragement and comfort you can share with them.

Chapter 3 Journal

4. What activity do you remember from childhood that brought smiles and joy to your life? Would you consider introducing that activity back into your life at this time?

Chapter 3 Exercise

Visualization Moment:

Set aside time and find a quiet place. Close your eyes and take some deep breaths. Now, visualize yourself as a young child. Picture your face and your expressions. What do you see? How do you feel? Go slow. Try feeling what your inner child is experiencing in that moment. Now, picture yourself as an adult taking that little child by the hand, giving them kindness and comfort. Allow them to express whatever is on their mind, reassuring them.

Chapter 3 Worksheet

Inner Child Dialogue:

- Describe a time in your childhood when you felt afraid, anxious, or hurt.

- Try to identify the emotions you felt during this experience.

- Write a note to your inner child about those moments of pain, giving them reassurance and comfort.

- List some ways to provide protection and care for your inner child moving forward.

Chapter 4

Releasing the Pain of Our Past

I decided early on in adulthood that I wanted to be a teacher and impact the lives of others. This career path led me to graduate studies focused on special needs students. This was a joyous time in my life. My husband and I were building our home together and creating ministry activities to help those in need. What we did not realize or understand during this stage of our lives was the effect that our childhood trauma had on us. This all changed when I received a phone call informing me that my mom, who had spent years in an abusive relationship with my stepfather, had committed suicide.

The devastation I felt emotionally was, at times, unbearable. My mom had finally reached her breaking point. During the grieving process that followed, I experienced trauma that was, at times, too much to manage. My stepfather had been held accountable in his life for criminal behavior and had spent a few years in prison. I was the one who encouraged my mom to reunite with this man who had changed, or at least I thought. Unfortunately, he had not. Upon his release from prison, he began living as he always had. My mom was victimized again. The difference was that I now felt responsible for her situation and untimely death. I was reliving those emotional trauma wounds from my childhood. I internalized the scars that my stepfather created as being the sole reason things had happened in my family's life. I was somehow to blame.

This chapter is entitled "Releasing the Pain of Our Past." We will discuss the importance of bottled-up emotions and present what I believe are effective strategies for overcoming the pain and abuse of our past. We will embrace vulnerability, learn how to face the trauma that is still residing in our mind and body, and provide the step-by-step process both my husband and I have used in our healing journey.

Embracing Vulnerability

We first need to look at a pair of crucial concept definitions that will help explain with greater clarity what is happening once we experience trauma, especially trauma from our childhood. They are:

- **Co-regulation:** refers to how one person helps another manage their emotional responses. In theory, this would be represented by a supportive caregiver who helps a child navigate feelings amid a traumatic event, providing comfort and reassurance and, most importantly, modeling healthy emotional regulation.

- **Self-regulation:** refers to how one person manages their emotions, responses, and behaviors during a trauma event. It plays a crucial role in how children learn to manage their feelings.

In my childhood, the caregivers in my life could not self-regulate. That created an environment that was toxic and unpredictable. It also confused my siblings and me due to our family's lack of emotional consistency. The long-term effects of being exposed to sexual abuse, physical abuse, emotional abuse, and domestic violence left us devoid as children of any healthy way to manage our emotions. Clinicians would say the impact of not having a modeled self-regulation by our parents would be:

- **An Insecure Attachment:** Because our parents were always stressed, overwhelmed, or in conflict, they could not consistently respond to us as children, which fostered an insecure attachment. We always lived with a sense of abandonment and were unable to trust. I grew up feeling insecure about any relationship I had, and this was a difficulty in the early years of my marriage.

- **Emotional Dysregulation:** Because we did not see healthy examples of coping mechanisms, we did not have a model to learn how to regulate our emotions. What we saw and learned was to react emotionally to any event, and we bottled up our emotions. We did not know how to identify and express our feelings.

- **Internalized Shame and Guilt:** Because I learned to internalize the emotions of not only my parents but also myself at an early age, I took on the blame for the things that were done to me. I was to blame; I was constantly needing to be a people pleaser, and I lived with a deep sense of shame for the trauma that was inflicted upon me.

- **Anxious and Hypervigilant:** My parents could not self-regulate, so our home was always unpredictable and often violent. I remained hypervigilant through all my years as an adolescent due to the unsafe environment.

- **Poor Self-Regulation Skills:** I had no tools to use when exposed to emotional ups and downs. I did not know how to deal with the stress around me, leading to poor decisions.

My takeaway from all this emotional regulation is that I never had a healthy response to emotional turmoil modeled for me. Thus, I needed to start on the path to releasing pain by providing self-compassion and self-care to myself and my past. It will take time for anyone to unlearn patterns created in childhood, and knowing that is what has happened in my life also provides me hope for your transformation. We are on the road to a healing journey. Let us learn from the past and begin rewriting our story.

Power to Confront the Trauma

We need to begin the healing process by learning to self-regulate emotions. Here are some of the best strategies for developing this much-needed tool of change:

- **Build Emotional Awareness:** We must recognize when our emotions spike. We should create a "time-out" for ourselves and respond thoughtfully and reflectively instead of immediately reacting. Write down what you are experiencing in a journal to slow down the tendency to react in the moment.

- **Practice Mindfulness:** This means a few things. Be aware of what is happening around you, do not judge what is happening as good or bad, accept the reality of the situation, and focus on your response. What helped me with this strategy was multifaceted. I used prayer and meditation for starters and incorporated elements of Zen meditation music and healing meditation music. This created a much calmer and more positive Melissa over time.

- **Learn Cognitive Reframing Skills:** View situations or circumstances from different perspectives. One area that resonated for my husband and me was when we approached underserved communities or what we would call "the least of these," we did so from the perspective of being wounded healers. Often, we would not be sure how to help, yet by offering the underserved a reframing of their situations, we saw positive results in their lives. And being wounded healers allowed us to reframe whatever difficulties we were facing.

- **Use Breathing and Relaxation Techniques:** While incorporating this strategy, numerous breathing and relaxation techniques exist. There is what is known as belly breathing, box breathing, 4-7-8 breathing, alternate nostril breathing, and more.

- **Setting Healthy Boundaries:** This strategy produces emotional safety. I did not learn how to define what is acceptable in relationships until I was an adult. Due to the dysfunction I exhibited as a child and into adolescence, this has been a life-long learning curve.

- **Develop Self-Compassion:** This has been a massive component of my healing process. I have invested extensively in my affirmations. I have reminded myself daily since beginning my healing journey that I matter.

- **Identify Physical Components:** I have spent the past few decades dedicated to physical activities that provide an outlet or a release of pent-up energy. I love to exercise, and this, along with good eating habits, has been a game-changer for me emotionally.

The list above shows strategies that can work in the healing journey. They create a calmer and better you and provide a more stable and secure emotional atmosphere than before implementing these activities. My husband and I would not have ventured far on our healing journey if we had not combined most of this into our daily routines. These strategies provided us with emotional health.

We next want to examine our central nervous system again since all feelings originate here. As we discussed earlier, there are two main components: the sympathetic nervous system (SNS) and the parasympathetic nervous system (PNS).

The SNS can be called the fight-or-flight-or-freeze-or-fawn system because it prepares our bodies for responses to perceived dangers or traumatic events in our past. When we sense any peril, the SNS becomes highly activated, resulting in a series of activities. These include our heart rate increasing and the quickening of breathing, increased blood flow to muscles, and the release of stress hormones like cortisol and adrenaline. We respond with one of the 4F responses depending on our underlying thought process. The most challenging aspect of activating this system is that the SNS can become highly sensitive over time, which keeps us primed to react instead of responding. We end up reacting to non-threatening situations when there is no need.

The PNS is known as the "rest and digest" system, and it provides a counterbalance for the SNS by calming the body under stress. When the PNS is activated, our heart rate and blood pressure are reduced, which promotes relaxation. Because of trauma in our past, it can become increasingly difficult to relax due to the possibility of triggers.

Combined, these two systems provide a balanced cycle when responding to stress and promoting a recovery process. The influx of trauma can disrupt this balance, however. As someone who spent years living with pain and abuse, it has not been easy to put away any heightened reactions to perceived threats. However, using strategies to address emotional self-regulation has been highly beneficial in providing traction toward healing.

So, what happens when we are confronted with a traumatic moment? I asked my husband to explain what occurred when he was faced with trauma at the golf course. This was when the dishwasher man attempted to molest him. The response he gave was that at the moment the attempted sexual assault was beginning, he physically ran out from the cellar, and with fear and confusion, he could see how his SNS had been activated. The trauma would not be processed, though. He was too young to self-regulate and did not have this modeled for him by his caregivers. The trauma, in essence, was being stored within him, unable to be understood or processed healthily. What he would experience for many years into adolescence and early adulthood were potential triggers for reliving those fearful moments. All it would take would be seeing an old golf course country club or someone who looked like the dishwasher man.

In my life, I spent decades holding inside the pain and abuse I was the recipient of during those moments of sexual assault. Whether it was molestation or the rape I endured, I could not escape the memory of the trauma that was being stored in my mind and body. All it took to trigger me was seeing a news report about a sexual crime or seeing something represented in a movie or television show that portrayed a similar event to my experience.

Knowing the trauma stayed with us was another light bulb moment for my husband and me. We could now clearly understand that our past events were dormant until triggered by something we heard or saw. As children, the trauma we were exposed to was far too powerful for us to process. This is where the defense mechanisms took center stage in our minds. We repressed many of those painful memories. We also utilized denial as a way to manage our feelings. My husband, as a child, would use imagination and fantasy not to face his trauma and his shame. The long-term effects of our defense mechanisms were detrimental to our development. However, we had no other strategy to use in overcoming the pain and abuse. So, we lived many years with trauma stored internally.

It was during my life coach training that I first learned the power of our emotional memory and how pain and abuse are stored within us until we take steps toward healing. For me, this began with the simple acknowledgment that I did have trauma internally that needed to be processed. We have all heard the famous maxim, "The first step in recovery is admitting there is a problem." My coaching mentor, Neecie, ensured I had this foundational step as a starting point for healing and change.

A Step-by-Step Process

The actual steps for working through my past were to examine the trauma and its effects on my life. I could not self-regulate, so I had to begin there. I had to start managing my ability to respond to triggers and the memories of my past more effectively. I had to admit that I had used different defense mechanisms in my life to counteract the trauma I had been exposed to. They were my salvation as a child since I could not face or process the feelings that were produced during those events. However, to move into recovery meant I had to understand the long-term effects of using those mechanisms. I also had to know that I had built emotional walls in my life that were fortresses of protection for me. Those walls not only kept me from feeling the pain and abuse of my past, but they also prevented me from discovering freedom from those emotions that were too hard to bear.

The next step was to begin trying to feel the pain from the past. This is the scariest aspect of the recovery process. I liken it to getting close to a fire. I love the warmth of a fire ring in the fall season. To experience the warmth, I have to get close to it. If I get too close, I get burned. This is how I saw my initial moments of feeling the pain of my past. I had to come alongside my inner child and provide comfort and assurance that we would not only get through the moments of reflection on those horrible events of the past but that we would come out of the recovery process with a sense of healing. And this is what has happened throughout my adult life. I have approached the painful memories slowly and carefully, allowing myself to experience the pain on my terms. And just like the cool fall nights and my warming up with that fire ring, I have allowed myself to touch those feelings more and more. What I have discovered is that each time I approach those feelings of pain, they have less and less power over me.

My husband and I have learned in our recovery process that we both needed to understand how to self-regulate our emotions. We have had to ensure we found what clinicians would call a "safe place" for us to process our thoughts and memories of trauma. We have learned that, as children, adolescents, and young adults, the only effective way we had to process the pain in our lives was by using defense mechanisms. And we had to trust that taking small, incremental steps toward those feelings of pain would lessen their power over our past, present, and future. The emotional walls we built early in our lives have fallen brick by brick. I believe all of us who have been impacted by childhood trauma hope there is some point in time when recovery will be complete. However, I have discovered that healing is not a destination but a journey. The beauty of recovery is experienced by taking one step at a time, one day at a time.

We next turn to those potentially paralyzing triggers that are reminders of the pain and abuse of our past. How do we implement an effective strategy to combat those moments?

Key Takeaways

- If our parents or caregivers could not self-regulate, we were left without any healthy response to managing our emotions as children.

- The healing process needs to begin with our work on being able to self-regulate.

- The bi-product of not being able to self-regulate produces insecure attachments.

- The sympathetic and parasympathetic systems provide cycles of regulating our emotional response to stress-related events; the influx of trauma disrupts this balanced state with heightened reactions to perceived stress.

- Trauma unaddressed in childhood becomes stored in the body.

- With no other alternative to addressing the stored-up trauma, we naturally turn to defense mechanisms for relief.

- By working on the development of self-regulation, we position ourselves to manage triggers, and the memories associated with them more effectively.

- The more often we approach the pain of the past, the less power it seems to have upon our lives.

Chapter 4 Journal

1. As a child, did you have caregivers who could self-regulate their emotions and who modeled that for you?

_____
_____
_____
_____
_____
_____
_____
_____
_____
_____
_____
_____
_____
_____
_____
_____
_____
_____
_____
_____
_____
_____
_____

Chapter 4 Journal

2. If you do not have self-regulation skills, which strategies for developing them would be most helpful to you now?

_____
_____
_____
_____
_____
_____
_____
_____
_____
_____
_____
_____
_____
_____
_____
_____
_____
_____
_____

Chapter 4 Journal

3. Think of a time when you were deeply upset or overwhelmed. What do you think triggered those feelings? Might that be something from your past?

Chapter 4 Journal

4. How do you think processing the pain of your past will help you grow as a person?

Chapter 4 Exercise

Visualization: Releasing the Weight:

Sit quietly and visualize yourself carrying a heavy backpack filled with rocks. Each rock represents a painful memory.

Imagine taking out a rock one by one, acknowledging its significance, and setting it aside—never to be put back in the backpack again.

Chapter 4 Worksheet

Affirmation Activity:

Negative thoughts of painPositive affirmation

I do not have a voice in my life	I have something valuable to share with others

Chapter 5
Managing Trauma Triggers

My husband worked at a manufacturing facility many years ago that required him to open the doors before 6:00 a.m. This meant he would leave our home between 5:00 and 5:30 each morning. A morning commute at that hour should be safe and non-eventful. Such was not the case. My husband often had fellow drivers who would tailgate no matter his driving speed, producing undue stress early in the morning. It also brought upon my husband flashbacks from an incident decades earlier. The lights on his back bumper triggered an emotional memory. To this day, he struggles with people driving at an unreasonably close distance to that event from his past. When the trigger began years ago, his response each morning was to turn his outside mirrors away from the cars behind him and to pull down the inside mirror so the view was not distracting. He discovered that this odd approach to driving each morning was extremely helpful. The bright lights in his rearview did not impair him, thus inducing a calmer drive to work.

The title of this chapter is "Managing Trauma Triggers." My goal is to define trauma triggers and provide a template for creating a trauma toolkit to help us become more aware of their potential, understand our responses to triggers, develop coping strategies, and learn how to navigate the trails of communication, especially with those closest to us relationally.

Defining Triggers

Technically, trauma triggers are involuntary responses that happen when one of our senses—such as a smell, a sound, or a visual—activates a memory or an emotion related to a past traumatic event. Triggers often bypass our consciousness, leading to overwhelming feelings, especially when compared to the present situation that has triggered the emotion. For example, I struggle today with people's voices that I consider loud, whether in a room or on a television. This is because they remind me of my stepfather's voice as a child. His tone was often loud, harsh, and abusive, which created a solid emotional imprint on me. The loud voices have no meaning for me in the present per se but take me back to those moments of fear and helplessness as a child.

Triggers like the headlights during my husband's morning commute or my struggle with loud voices stem from the brain's encoding of trauma from our past. This occurs in the amygdala, the brain's emotional center. The amygdala is the part of our brain that detects outside threats and stores emotional memory. When trauma occurs, the brain records the event and creates a heightened sensitivity to the source of the trauma. This hyper-sensitivity, though needed now, can lead to chronic reactivity in adulthood. This is why we must learn to identify triggers and their origin. How else can we break free from their hold on us?

When our body responds to triggers, it does so with activity from our sympathetic nervous system (SNS). Remember from the previous chapter that our heart rate and breathing quicken, blood flow to muscles increases, and our body releases stress hormones like cortisol and adrenaline. This prepares us for fight-or-flight-or-freeze-or-fawn responses. So, for us as survivors of trauma, whether the event is an actual threat or not, our body senses that it is. The parasympathetic (PNS) system, responsible for calming our body down, struggles to counteract the overreaction to the event.

An example of what this looks like would be from my husband's past. He struggled with emotional dysregulation in his adolescent and early adult years. As a young adult, he worked on his undergraduate degree. While doing so, he enrolled in classes that required public speaking at various intervals during the semester. This terrified him. He found that he was getting stuck in cycles of hyperarousal (e.g., anxiety) or hypoarousal (e.g., disconnection). This not only made it difficult for him to process in the moment but also perpetuated his childhood patterns of avoidance coping mechanisms. What he experienced as "stage fright" was a response to his past. The good news is that he never stopped working on this. Today, he will speak in front of an audience with little or no reactions to the underlying SNS response his body activates.

Creating a Trauma Toolkit

The keys to overcoming the impact of triggers at the moment lie in our preparation work. While the body's response to triggers is designed to protect us from danger, we must take steps to reduce the emotional overload, if you will, of our responses. This leads us back to the strategies for self-regulating that we introduced in the last chapter. We must remember that triggers are cues that bring back memories tied to past trauma. For us as survivors of childhood abuse, these triggers typically disrupt our emotional regulation. Our goals must include understanding the states I mentioned above when discussing my husband, his inability to handle public speaking in college, and his breaking free from those patterns developed in childhood. The two states of potential perceived threat include:

- **Hyperarousal:** This is the fight-or-flight response and is characterized by panic and anxiety. Symptoms include a rapid heartbeat, sweating, and an inability to focus. In this state, minor stressors can seem impossible.

- **Hypoarousal:** In this state, the freeze response leads to dissociation, detachment, and emotional numbness.

So, how do we build a trauma trigger toolbox that will help us navigate the daily challenges we face? What strategies can we incorporate? Whatever we do must be directed toward helping us in short-term immediate responses and long-term healing objectives for our lives. Some of the most effective approaches, according to clinicians, are:

- **Grounding Exercises:** These are our go-to exercises in an emergency overload. Instead of feeling overwhelmed and unable to move, we should be able to rely on the breathing exercises mentioned in Chapter 4. We should also be aware of what therapists call the 5-4-3-2-1 technique. This involves acknowledging five things you can see, four things you can touch, three things you can hear, two things you can smell, and one thing you can taste. This technique works because it interrupts the negative thought cycles racing in our minds during the triggering moment. It refocuses mental energy.

- **Mindfulness Techniques:** Practicing mindfulness is a key to living a more peaceful and less reactionary life. Prayer, meditation, music, and reflection can encourage us to observe our thoughts and feelings without judgment, which can reduce reactivity to triggers. These activities aim to cultivate a sense of safety and provide self-compassion and self-care.

- **Emotional Resilience:** We can lessen the impact of our emotions by naming them (e.g., "I feel panic"). At the very least, this can reduce the intensity of the moment.

- **Journaling:** Also, writing about triggers can help us understand which areas of our lives are most impacted. We may discover patterns of behavior that will better equip us for any potential triggers.

- **Creating a Safe Place:** This has become vital to my life. I aim to create a physically and emotionally safe place in my home for managing triggers—a place where things like lighting and scents are a priority. Also, creating a safe place means establishing healthy boundaries in all my relationships.

- **Physical Activity:** Exercise has had a profound effect on my life. It has reduced stress hormones immensely and appears to help me regulate my nervous system better. I feel so much more in control of my life when I have worked to expend all the pent-up energy in my body.

- **Cognitive-Behavioral Therapy Strategies:** CBT-based techniques focus on identifying and reframing the negative thought patterns that can be associated with trauma-based triggers. If changed, my perception of an event will alter what I think, feel, and respond to the event.

- **Build a Supportive Network:** This can include a few people. For several years, only my husband and I provided trust, validation, and understanding for each other. The key is having someone who can co-regulate with you and help soothe your nervous system. Support groups can be vital in this aspect of our healing.

- **Develop a trigger plan:** Proactively identifying and preparing for triggers can reduce their power over our lives. Journaling what trips us, what responses to triggers have or have not worked, and creating lists of affirmations all need to be in our toolkit.

Understanding Our Responses

By consistently practicing these coping strategies, we can gradually reduce the intensity of our reactions to triggers and build a sense of empowerment over our physiological and emotional responses to any event.

Understanding and managing triggers is an essential part of the healing process. Triggers, my biggest enemy over the years, can disrupt many aspects of our lives. They can create emotional disruption, bring back the pain and abuse of our past, and generate obstacles in our day-to-day. We can reduce their hold on our lives, though. We must remember again that healing is a journey, not a destination. Healing is not a solitary journey, however. The support of loved ones or a support group can make a profound difference. Communication is critical in helping those closest to us understand what we are going through. Let's learn how to share our experiences, fostering a sense of connection rather than isolation. I know firsthand that it is difficult when we first attempt to share with others, but this is the path to strengthening our capacity for self-regulation and healing.

Triggers are not the definition of who we are. They are part of our story, the story we are working to rewrite, which will eventually reflect resilience, hope, and empowerment. We now need to begin discussing a vital aspect of our growth: learning how to forgive those who have violated us—not for their sake but for our own.

Key Takeaways

- Triggers often bypass our conscience, leading to overwhelming feelings.

- The amygdala is the brain's emotional center. This part of our brain detects outside threats and stores emotional memory.

- The key to effective responses to triggers is in our preparation work. We need to take steps to reduce the level of emotional overload we experience.

- We must consider our strategies' short-term and long-term effects to manage our triggers.

- Understanding and managing triggers is essential to the healing process.

- Healing is a journey, not a destination.

- Healing is not a solitary journey. We need support and encouragement along the way.

Chapter 5 Journal

1. What are the most common situations, people, or places that make me feel emotionally overwhelmed or unsafe?

___

Chapter 5 Journal

2. What physical sensations do I notice in my body when triggered?

_____
_____
_____
_____
_____
_____
_____
_____
_____
_____
_____
_____
_____
_____
_____
_____
_____
_____
_____

Chapter 5 Journal

3. What are the recurring thoughts or emotions I experience when triggered? What events in my past do they recall?

Chapter 5 Journal

4. How can I create a place or situation where I feel completely calm and safe?

Chapter 5 Exercise

Trigger Creation Exercise:

Write down a list of your known triggers. For each one, note:

- The event or situation that triggers it.

- Your emotional reaction.

- Your physical sensations.

- Reflect on why these are most challenging.

Chapter 5 Worksheet

Calm and Safe Planning Tool:

The objective here is to create a personalized plan to manage triggers. You should look at the following ideas:

- Identify a grounding technique(s) you can use in real-time.

- Describe a calming environment you can retreat to.

- Write a comforting affirmation or mantra for yourself.

- List anyone you can talk to when overwhelmed.

- Develop a step-by-step plan for the next trigger experience.

Chapter 6

The Power of Forgiveness

The years after my mom's suicide were extremely difficult for me. I had been victimized by my stepfather sexually and by his domestic violence toward our family, especially my mom, while growing up. I learned to hate this man, and yet I considered myself a Christian woman. I could not get past the pain he had caused and the feelings I held so tightly. I could say I forgive him, but those were only words. What I often misunderstood about forgiveness was that it required me to ensure my stepfather's actions no longer held power or influence over my life.

This chapter's title is "The Power of Forgiveness." In it, we will examine the idea that forgiveness is not only aimed at those who have harmed us but also that we need to forgive ourselves for past wrongs. Finally, we will examine the power of forgiveness. It can change who we are as individuals and how we move forward.

Forgiveness is a Choice

First and foremost, we must understand that forgiveness is a choice. It is an intentional act that requires conscious effort and a willingness to let go of the emotions that past wrongs have created. In my stepfather's case, this would take me a few decades. It took a long time for me to understand that forgiveness was not letting my stepfather off the hook for what he had done to all of us as a family. It was reclaiming, for me, emotional freedom.

One of the misconceptions about forgiveness is that it requires forgetting or excusing what has happened in our lives. Nothing could be further from the truth. True forgiveness is not about ignoring the pain. It is about choosing to stop holding onto it. When we forgive, we are acknowledging the trauma that occurred and that it was, and often still is, painful. We do not forget what has happened to us, but instead let go of the bitterness, resentment, and anger. This is hard to do.

Forgiveness is ultimately about being freed from the pain and abuse of the past. It is an act of self-liberation that allows us to take back control over our lives. Imagine a world where our thoughts and emotions are no longer enslaved to the one(s) who perpetrated against us, a world where the chains of bondage to our past no longer define us. This can be empowering because it shifts the focus from the person who harmed us to taking charge of our emotional health.

Forgiveness is a Process

Forgiveness must also be seen as a process and not a one-time event. It requires time, in some cases, a very long time. At least it did for me. I would go months, even years, with a sense of forgiveness in my heart for my stepfather. I would then be triggered concerning my mom, and my memory of her and the bitterness toward my stepfather would ensue again. Many therapists would say there are multiple stages to this process of forgiveness. Those stages would include:

- Recognition of the pain
- Acknowledgement of the hurt caused
- Gradual acceptance that we cannot change the past

In my case, it has always required me to revisit my feelings of anger and bitterness, learn to process the emotions over and over again, and then make the choice of letting go of the pain.

Forgiveness, like all trauma-related events, is about reframing the past, examining the underlying issues again, and committing to forgiving those who have wronged us.

The irony in what I am sharing is that forgiveness is a gift to yourself. In my case, it is a gift to me. By choosing to forgive the one who has violated us, we are moving toward peace with the past instead of living in the pain and despair that holding grudges produces. What about resentment and letting go of the past?

Resentment was an emotional prison for me from early adulthood into middle age. During those years, I felt justified to hate the man who had destroyed our family. I could never get beyond those thoughts and live in the moment consistently. I was always looking back and reliving the pain.

Strategies for Forgiveness

So, how do we release the pain of those memories and forgive those who have wronged us? It should come as no surprise that the ingredients for self-regulation are the same strategies for helping us work through unforgiveness. The most potent methods for releasing the pain are practicing mindfulness, creating safe places to process the pain, and having self-compassion and self-care.

We looked at the elements of self-regulation in the previous chapter. Practicing mindfulness, for me, involves prayer and meditation; it requires scripture reading and focuses on music and reflection. These activities cultivate a sense of peace in me. They help me become less reactive and more responsive to triggers and the world around me. Creating a safe place means setting boundaries that provide healthy relationships. Self-compassion and self-care ensure I am patient and mindful of what is in my best interests as I work through my feelings.

The Importance of Forgiving Ourselves

Forgiveness is not just for those who have offended us. It is also a trait we must exhibit toward ourselves. Self-forgiveness, for me, has been one of the most powerful tools in my emotional healing process. I mentioned earlier in the book how I took ownership of the blame for my childhood trauma. Again, I think more than anything, if I was at fault, I could still hold onto the idea that my parents would eventually be there for us. If, however, I resigned myself to the notion that our parents were to blame, hopelessness would be my lot in life. Thus, I blamed myself for the trauma in our family or at least for the abuse I received.

Self-blame was a constant in my life during adolescence and early adulthood. I have experienced it on occasion since. There are multiple problems with this trait. For starters, it keeps us anchored thoroughly in the past, unable to move forward. We struggle to be ourselves as a result. Even though guilt can be a healthy component of our lives, when we have it in excess, it can become toxic. It inevitably diminishes our sense of self-worth, where we define ourselves by the mistakes in our lives. I can trace every element of negative self-talk to those emotions tied to blame, shame, and guilt. To break this cycle, I have learned over the years to replace the criticism of myself with compassion and affirmation. I have had to learn to be kind to myself and express this in the many journals I have kept and on those precious sticky notes. Thinking about the sticky notes does make me smile. As I said earlier, they are everywhere at home and work.

Cultivating kindness and compassion for ourselves is a good thing, too. We often allow pride or indifference to get in the way, but we develop a more holistic view of ourselves by being kind to ourselves. If someone we loved struggled with these same issues, we would quickly remind them of their worth, strengths, and value. We need to do the same for ourselves when we fall short. Whether through journaling, affirmations, or mindfulness techniques, let us always remember to incorporate self-compassion and kindness into our daily routines.

My husband's daily responsibilities at work include ensuring products are manufactured promptly, efficiently, and profitably. He would say that when one of his employees committed a snafu and made a sizable mistake, it was not about fault-finding at the moment. What it was about was creating process improvements, as he calls them. His point of view would be to discover how the mistake happened, create a better process, and then train the staff to incorporate change into their daily work habits. He never found fault with the people but instead with the process. This has stuck with me as I have sorted through my struggles with self-blame. I have tried to follow his mantra. Let's create a better process and live by it moving forward. The rewards far outweigh the effort needed for change.

The Power of Forgiveness

We have discussed the need for forgiveness for those who have violated us and for us to forgive ourselves. But there is something more to this thing called forgiveness. It has the power to change not only circumstances but the culture around us as well. My husband volunteered for a few years with an organization whose mission is to restore victims and offenders in the criminal justice system. He will never forget hearing the story of a young lady who had been shot. Her experience was heart-wrenching. What was more impressive, however, is that the shooter had been reconciled to her. How is that even possible? Their story is more than inspiring; it has changed countless lives since. In this case, the ripple effect of the victim forgiving the shooter, followed by reconciliation, is still helping to transform the emotional climate of their families and community.

In sum, forgiveness fosters a culture of empathy and compassion; it reduces toxicity, promotes emotional healing and health, builds trust, and strengthens relationships. Forgiveness makes the world a better place. Forgiveness has been paramount as I have traversed the proverbial landscape of trying to understand it. I know that being forgiven for a wrong is one of the most valuable gifts I have been given. Wading through the difficulty of forgiving my stepfather for his actions toward our family has provided the most incredible sense of freedom I could ever know. It has become one of the essential self-care acts during my healing journey. Will I spend the rest of my life remembering the difficulties my mom endured? The answer is yes. I will also not forget the little things she did to try and make my life better amid those moments of childhood trauma. Forgiveness has given me freedom from the pain of the past. May it do the same for you.

Next, we turn to the various treatment modalities available to those seeking professional support and guidance.

Key Takeaways

- Forgiveness is a choice we make. It is an intentional act that requires conscious effort and a willingness to let go of the emotions that past wrongs have created.

- Forgiveness allows freedom from the pain and abuse of the past.

- Forgiveness shifts the focus from the offending person who harmed us having control over our lives; instead, forgiveness allows us to take charge of our emotional health.

- Many therapists see forgiveness through the lens of a process. This process includes recognizing the pain, acknowledging the hurt caused, and gradually accepting the offense.

- The most potent methods for releasing the pain are practicing mindfulness, creating safe places to process it, and having self-care and self-compassion.

- Forgiveness fosters a culture of empathy and compassion.

- Forgiveness reduces toxicity, promotes emotional healing, builds trust, and strengthens relationships.

Chapter 6 Journal

1. What does forgiveness mean to you personally? How have your experiences with trauma shaped this definition?

_____
_____
_____
_____
_____
_____
_____
_____
_____
_____
_____
_____
_____
_____
_____
_____
_____
_____
_____
_____

Chapter 6 Journal

2. Do you struggle to forgive people, situations, or aspects of yourself?

___

Chapter 6 Journal

3. How has holding onto resentment, anger, or hurt affected your mental, emotional, and physical health?

_____
_____
_____
_____
_____
_____
_____
_____
_____
_____
_____
_____
_____
_____
_____
_____
_____
_____
_____
_____
_____

Chapter 6 Journal

4. What aspects of your past do you feel guilty or ashamed of? How might forgiving yourself for these feelings support your healing journey?

Chapter 6 Exercise

The Letter:

Is there someone you need to forgive? Write them a letter and be honest about how their actions affected you, but you now want to forgive them. Once finished, tear up the letter, symbolically emphasizing how you are letting go of the resentment you have held in your heart toward them.

RESTORING THE BROKEN PIECES

Chapter 6 Worksheet

Forgiveness Reflection:

This worksheet is designed to help you understand your thoughts and emotions about a need for forgiveness.

- What happened? Describe the event or the situation.

- How did it affect me? Reflect on the emotional, physical, and relational impact.

- Why forgive? List reasons why forgiveness might benefit you.

- Next steps: Outline action steps you can take toward forgiveness.

Chapter 7
Seeking Professional Support

In the introduction to this book, I mentioned that I thought the audience for this work would be individuals who knew they needed to address underlying issues from their past but were not ready or able to seek professional help or support. To that end, I want to share what the prevailing treatment modalities for the healing of childhood trauma are. I am not a therapist but a life coach. Thus, I am not familiar with many of the modalities we are about to discuss. However, I am a survivor of pain and abuse from the past and have worked through my trauma with a pair of these means of treatment. Between my self-help journey and utilizing trained professionals, I have come to thrive in this stage of my life.

The need to seek professional help for childhood trauma is not only beneficial but, for many, it is essential for long-term recovery. Because I left trauma unaddressed as an adolescent and into early adulthood, I experienced a variety of emotional and psychological challenges that negatively impacted me. I struggled with anxiety, depression, guilt, and shame. These unresolved feelings affected my relationships, including my marriage. It was hard to develop trust in others that would lead to healthy emotional connections. Additionally, from my adolescence, I turned to unhealthy coping mechanisms in an attempt to manage the overwhelming emotions tied to my past.

The Value of Therapy

Therapists and mental health professionals provide a thorough, structured, compassionate healing approach. One of the most vital aspects of seeking professional support is that therapy can occur in a safe and confidential environment. A setting like that allows individuals to confront painful memories at their own pace, yet always with someone who empathizes and understands. Through therapy with a professional, individuals can develop far healthier self-perceptions and more effective ways of managing stress and relationships. Moreover, therapy can offer a toolkit of coping strategies to use in day-to-day life to reduce the emotional weight of trauma. Among the tools therapy provides is learning to recognize negative thought patterns, reframing those patterns, and potentially building a support system. With proper treatment, individuals can rebuild their self-worth and create emotionally healthy lives. Remember, therapy is not just about healing but is more about empowering those of us who have waded through the pain and abuse of our past to live with resilience and hope for the future. Here are some of the different therapies used for treating trauma:

Therapeutic Modalities

- **Cognitive Behavioral Therapy (CBT):** This particular psychotherapy seeks to correct cognitive distortions. The goal is to alter thoughts, beliefs, attitudes, and associated behaviors. The result is improved emotional regulation and developing coping strategies that address issues in an individual's life. CBT has several core principles that include the idea that most problems are based, at least in part, on faulty thinking, that treatment involves efforts to change these thinking patterns, and that learning better ways to cope will relieve symptoms of problematic behavior. For those impacted by childhood trauma, CBT helps to correct negative beliefs and provide a more balanced and compassionate perspective.

- **Cognitive Processing Therapy (CPT):** This is a form of CBT that is designed primarily for trauma survivors. The treatment of PTSD is associated with this modality. CPT emphasizes how trauma shapes an individual's belief about safety, trust, self-esteem, and control. CPT is aimed at those "stuck points" in an individual's life, such as "it was my fault." The cognitive restructuring is more specific to trauma-related events with CPT. The fundamental differences between CBT and CPT revolve around the focus on underlying issues and the particular techniques used in therapy.

- **Prolonged Exposure Therapy (PE):** This is another form of cognitive therapy that was designed to treat PTSD. Two main treatment procedures characterize it. It is focused on retelling traumatic memories. The second involves exposure to situations, places, and things that are reminders of the trauma. The fundamental difference with PE is that it emphasizes exposure to past trauma versus a shift in cognitive distortions as the focus.

- **Eye Movement Desensitization & Reprocessing (EMDR):** This form of therapy helps an individual become less sensitive to trauma memories by recalling and reliving the experience in a safe and therapeutic environment. The underlying premise is that trauma can be reprocessed and reframed by the brain using primarily bilateral stimulation, with eye movements being the predominant means. A therapist may also use sounds to help an individual reprocess the event of trauma.

- **Trauma-Focused CBT (TF-CBT):** Here is another form of CBT. The fundamental difference with TF-CBT is that it was created for use with children and adolescents impacted by trauma. TF-CBT also seeks to involve the caregivers as integral participants. An additional component is the skills integrated by TF-CBT that are in place to manage child-specific behavioral challenges.

- **Somatic Therapy:** This approach to therapy focuses on the connection between the mind and body to alleviate unresolved trauma and the resultant emotional pain. Unlike the talk therapies above, which focus primarily on cognitive and emotional processes, somatic therapy emphasizes the physiological imprints of trauma. The benefits include a reduction of physical symptoms of trauma, the improvement of emotional regulation, and an enhancement of self-awareness. The work addresses the trauma with nonverbal memories.

- **Dialectical Behavior Therapy (DBT):** is another form of CBT. DBT was developed to help address intense emotional challenges, self-destructive behaviors, and interpersonal difficulties. Much of the literature revolves around DBT's emphasis on validation and mindfulness to target individuals who struggle with pervasive emotional dysregulation. DBT seeks the notion that individuals need to be able to accept themselves and their circumstances.

- **Internal Family Systems Therapy (IFS):** This model focuses on how an individual can understand and harmonize the different parts of themselves. What is meant by various parts is that the mind is seen as a system of sub-personalities. Each of these parts represents distinct beliefs and feelings, every one of which may carry traumatic memories. The categories for the different parts are the exiles who carry the trauma, managers who use defenses to protect against the pain, and firefighters who take extreme measures to protect us when pain surfaces. At the core of the IFS is the "self," which can lead and heal all the other parts. The self is part of the individual who brings confidence and calmness. The goal of therapy is to help us connect with the self.

- **Narrative Exposure Therapy (NET):** This treatment focuses on helping individuals contextualize traumatic events within the broader framework of their lives. It does involve the processing of emotions tied to past trauma, but it also focuses on the entire life narrative. This would provide an individual with a testimony about their resilience and progress from the past over time. This does not address individual traumas as much as creating a big-picture recap of their lives.

Additional modalities can be listed, and informational websites will be included in the book's reference section. The takeaway for me is that there are many different forms of treatment available to those who have experienced childhood trauma. No matter what the modality is, the goal of all types of trauma therapies is to create a safe and supportive environment where we can work through all the pain and abuse in our past.

The Impact of Support and Encouragement

I want to mention an additional aspect of treating trauma. One that has been highly beneficial to me. It is taking part in either group therapy or peer support groups. I have participated in both. What has been most encouraging in my recovery process has been having a shared experience with others like me. Knowing that other people are in my shoes, so to speak, has been an impetus for my healing.

Healing from childhood trauma is such a profound journey. When I look back and realize how little I understood about my past and its impact on my present-day living, I wonder why I never sought help sooner. The trauma I have experienced in my life has shaped me. The thoughts I had for many years, the emotions I carried, and the impact on my relationships were far-reaching. I have written this book for those who need a self-help guide for their life. While self-help strategies are valuable, as they have been in my life, a professional therapeutic experience can offer a more structured and informed approach to addressing all the underlying layers of pain and dysfunction left by trauma.

A trusted therapist, or in my case, a trusted therapist who was guiding us through life coaching protocol, proved essential to my understanding of trauma itself. I now see that the safe and non-judgmental environment she created for those who needed to work through our past was crucial as we revisited painful memories and emotions. I know that for many of us trying to make a recovery journey, the most critical aspect will be learning how to trust another person with our past. Many of us have been betrayed too often to enter into a relationship about our pain. We need to remind ourselves that choosing a therapist is an act of empowerment. It signals a willingness on our part to confront the past and reclaim control over our lives. With the proper professional support, our healing journey becomes less and less isolating, paving the way for connection, authenticity, and trust. Trusting a therapist is not just a step toward healing – it is a statement that we are ready to thrive.

Taking Ownership of Our Recovery

If you are beginning your self-help journey, I encourage you to take ownership of your healing process. Simply gaining knowledge about trauma and its effects allows you to better understand the connection between your past and present challenges. This alone will help you, as it did me, reduce the blame, shame, and guilt of our past. Additionally, it can foster self-compassion and self-care. These traits open a floodgate for change.

Practicing self-help techniques, such as journaling, mindfulness techniques, and breathing exercises, can promote relief and emotional regulation. This helps us stay in the moment and not be trapped in the pain and abuse of our past. A self-help journey also reinforces the belief that change and healing are possible. While it does not replace professional support and therapy, it lays a strong foundation for our healing journey. By taking these steps, we demonstrate to ourselves that we are committed to reclaiming our lives from the grips of past trauma. It affirms the strength and hope inherent in your lives and mine.

We are now ready to create a fully organized plan for beginning action steps on our healing journey. We turn to that next.

Key Takeaways

- The key to long-term recovery for many revolves around working with a therapist.

- Therapists and mental health professionals provide a thorough, structured, compassionate healing approach.

- Therapy can offer a sizable range of strategic options for reducing the day-to-day emotional weight of trauma.

- Therapy can potentially provide a support group option where we can secure a shared experience with others going through recovery.

- A therapeutic modality ensures we are less and less isolated during our healing journey. This allows for relational connectivity, authenticity, and trust.

- It is important to take ownership of our healing process. We need to gain knowledge about trauma so we can better understand the connections between our past and present states.

Chapter 7 Journal

1. Reflect on the emotions that arise when you think about starting a self-help journey. What fears, hopes, or doubts come to mind?

_____
_____
_____
_____
_____
_____
_____
_____
_____
_____
_____
_____
_____
_____
_____
_____
_____
_____
_____

Chapter 7 Journal

2. What areas of your life do you hope to improve by engaging in a self-help practice? Why are these changes important to you?

_____
_____
_____
_____
_____
_____
_____
_____
_____
_____
_____
_____
_____
_____
_____
_____
_____
_____
_____
_____

Chapter 7 Journal

3. What small, achievable steps can you take this week to continue progressing your self-help journey?

_____
_____
_____
_____
_____
_____
_____
_____
_____
_____
_____
_____
_____
_____
_____
_____
_____
_____
_____
_____

Chapter 7 Journal

4. Imagine your life five years from now after consistent self-help efforts. How does it look different from today?

Chapter 7 Exercise

Creating a Self-Care Plan:

- Objective: Establish a personalized self-care routine to nurture your emotional well-being.

- Steps:

  1. Identify 3 activities that bring you comfort or joy.

     (e.g., journaling, walking, meditating)

  2. Schedule a specific time for each activity in the coming week.

  3. Reflect daily on how these practices affect your mood.

- Outcome: A structured routine that promotes grounding.

Chapter 7 Worksheet

Identifying Strengths and Resources:

- Objective: Recognize internal and external resources available for your healing journey.
- Sections:
  1. List 5 personal strengths (e.g., resilience, empathy, creativity).
  2. Identify 3 supportive people in your life.
  3. Write down 3 tools or practices (e.g., mindfulness techniques, Books, apps) that you can incorporate.

- Reflection: How can these strengths and resources support you?

- Seeking Support: What steps can you take to seek professional support?

Chapter 8
Writing Our New Narrative

Most people have seen the movie Forest Gump. My husband often tells others that Forest's girlfriend, Jenny, portrayed my life in the film. I see many similarities to my past when I think about her character. More importantly, I can connect with her story of redemption. She faced trauma, abuse, and pain, all of which lingered into adolescence and early adulthood. And yet, her story does not end there. It culminates in her search for a new life that brings change and restoration. A life that has meaning and purpose. That's my story, too. Hopefully, it is, or soon will be, yours as well.

We now come to our capstone chapter, "Writing Our New Narrative." I want to explore what it looks like to assemble all the puzzle pieces of a self-help healing journey. I will retrace the steps I took in the recovery process as an example of possible change.

I was aged 25 when I came to a breaking point in life. I was in Las Vegas and knew I did not have to live anymore like I had the previous decade. My life had spun out of control due to my inability to process the pain and abuse of the past. I had used coping mechanisms my entire life and had turned to substance use as a way to no longer face or feel the trauma I had experienced. My life was a mess.

When I flew back home, I knew I needed to seek intervention or find some help. Before leaving for Vegas, I had checked into a detox center only to walk out before actually receiving treatment. Upon returning home, I decided I would give the center another chance. I was denied entry, though. I was considered a "runner" and no longer eligible for their program. In that moment of rejection, there was such a sense of helplessness. What happened next is why I am writing this book.

On the counter at the detox was a pamphlet for a transitional house for women. I took the pamphlet and called the number inside to determine if I could enter their program. I was told there was one bed left. I immediately had my biological dad drop me off. He and I had begun working on our relationship during this time of my life. I will never forget his words when we drove to the transitional house. "Lisa, you don't have to do this." In my heart, though, I knew I had to. There is a time in every recovery process that beckons a call we cannot deny. Such was mine that day.

As I entered the house, I met the Director. Her name was Nadine, and I believe I would never have made it through my healing journey without her. She took me in as her daughter and began teaching me about the cycles of abuse. I knew in my heart she was right. I also told myself in those early days there that even though I was not responsible for the cycles of abuse I had been exposed to, those same cycles could, and would, end with me.

The day I entered the transitional home began what has now been a lifelong quest for healing. I have seen my life transformed in the years since. I remember just getting clean and sober for the first time. I also began talking through parts of my past. I then secured a job at a local cafeteria and started riding the bus daily to and from work. In the subsequent years, I would find freedom from the past, get married, earn a graduate degree, occupy a career with special needs students, form a marriage and family ministry, and have the opportunity to share with others who are further back down the recovery road. Yes, recovery is possible. So, where did the healing process from the childhood trauma begin for me?

Acknowledging the Pain and Enlisting Support

The first step in any recovery or healing process is to begin by acknowledging the pain and abuse we hold within. We must not accept being defined by our past. Instead, we must shift our perspective from being the victim, which we are, to becoming a survivor. This first step empowers us to initiate change for the future. In writing a new narrative for our lives, we must also come to terms with an understanding that the past cannot be changed. However, we do have the ability to decide how we are going to respond to those memories of trauma. This transforms how we view our present state as well as our future.

In my healing journey, the next step was to see the value of a support group or person. In the early stages of recovery, I had Nadine and my fellow housemates. Since that time, I have had my husband as well as individuals in my inner circle who were also on the road to recovery. All of us need someone who will rally around us during this stage of healing. Having other people who understand and support us is invaluable. I think of scripture when this topic comes to mind. The biblical writer of the book of Ecclesiastes wrote, *"Two are better than one, because they have a good return for their labor. If either of them falls, one can help the other up. But pity anyone who falls and has no one to help them up."* (Ecc. 4:9-10)

One of the benefits of having a support group or person in place is the help they can provide in reminding us of our worth. The beliefs I carried around inside my head for years included phrases like "I'm not worthy," "I can't trust others," "I'm not lovable," and other expressions that constantly reminded me I did not have a voice and I did not matter. While writing a new narrative, we should look at the past from a different perspective. One that doesn't deny the impact trauma has had upon us but instead celebrates the fact we have survived, shown resilience, and can build a better life beginning today. Writing a new narrative takes work. Thus, there is a need for support and encouragement. A new narrative helps us by reframing the past. We want to begin seeing ourselves through a new lens. A lens that sees what's possible in our lives. This is about awareness. So, how has our past shaped our thoughts, feelings, and behaviors?

Doing the Inner Child Work

What I did not know about the effects of trauma early on in recovery was the impact those events would have on my inner child – the part of me that held all of those emotions and experiences from my childhood. I learned the inner child concept from my mentor and life coach trainer, Dr. Neecie Moore. As a therapist, she was experienced at ensuring those of us who had childhood trauma were able to not only acknowledge the pain but also how to replace it with kindness, compassion, and care for our inner selves. Writing a new narrative must include creating a story that honors our inner child. As we continue to mend the brokenness of our past, we nurture the wounds we have long held onto and seek to heal through a provision of love and security for ourselves. What we should have been given in our youth by our caregivers is what we should strive to honor our lives with as adults. So, what does it look like to celebrate your inner child?

The first step to doing inner child work, at least in my story, was to think about the traumatic events I had experienced as a child. I needed to remember who I was during those events. What age, where was I, and if possible, what was I feeling? I found a comfortable place in my home to get alone and be still. I then would visualize Melissa or little Lisa as I was called, not directly in the moment of trauma, but right after, and come alongside her. I focused on what she looked like, her facial expressions, and how I could make this moment a safe place for her. I sought to connect with my younger self in that moment and be present for anything she might say or anything she might be feeling that I could perceive. I would then begin heaping upon her the comfort, the safety, and the affirmations I so desperately needed as little Lisa. As I felt her being consoled, I knew I was bringing about healing, at least for that time in my life. I would then end the session and provide myself with self-care and self-compassion. The initial thought of doing this seemed a bit weird. That said, I cannot overstate the value of these moments in my healing process. I had numerous events that would be considered adverse childhood experiences. So, meeting my inner child at various ages of my youth took quite a bit of time, and these moments were emotionally draining. But they also provided healing and hope. I am so thankful.

I think the next activity, or at least something that should be in place for survivors, is learning about childhood trauma. There are many excellent resources available to educate us on the impact of past trauma. I have created a resource here that introduces the subject and can serve as a bridge to more academic works. Plus, online counseling sites can serve as tools for learning and growing our knowledge of trauma and its treatment.

Releasing the Pain

Earlier in the book, I followed up the chapter on the inner child with one on releasing the pain of our past. Doing inner child work is releasing the pain. However, I want to ensure we distinguish between the two. If you remember, releasing pain has to start with an understanding of how we have learned to experience our emotions early in life. If our parents or caregivers could not self-regulate, we did not have a model to follow. Instead, we would have naturally recoiled from the trauma in our lives and used various defense mechanisms to ensure we didn't feel the emotions produced as a result of the event(s). This pattern follows us into adolescence and adulthood if we never process it. We continue to build walls to protect us from the hurt. Learning to self-regulate then becomes the key to unlearning those emotional habits and breaking down those emotional walls.

The most effective way to learn how to self-regulate is through the strategies mentioned in Chapter 4. Included were the ideas of building emotional awareness when we could create a time out for ourselves, take a deep breath, and remind ourselves that this is not the result of what is happening in the present. Instead, this triggering episode is a reminder of something in our past. Even more critical for me was, and continues to be, mindfulness practice. I have used prayer, meditation, scripture reading, and the incorporation of music therapy. I have benefited by becoming much more relaxed in my day-to-day life, which ensures less impact on me by those emotional triggers. I have also benefited from reframing my perspective about myself and my past. You can do the same. Other strategies could include:

- Setting healthy boundaries in relationships.
- Developing a proactive and intentional form of self-compassion and self-care.
- Breathing exercises.

The goal is to provide oneself with a calmer and better persona. This establishes a more stable and secure emotional climate for us each day.

Before moving on with our response to triggers in life, I want to remind you of the importance of bathing our hearts with the love and compassion we deserve. This was initially difficult because of my low self-esteem and self-worth. I struggled with the idea that I needed to be valued and cherished. But we all need to be cared for. What does this mean in practical terms? It means practicing self-compassion. We must treat ourselves like we would a dear friend or a cherished loved one. Trauma does not define any of us. It is what happened to us. We can heal from the pain and abuse of our past.

We also need to provide ourselves with a safe place in our relationships. This begins with creating healthy boundaries. We need to learn how to say no. We must remind ourselves that it may feel awkward or selfish, but it is in our best interests. I was a people pleaser, so saying no was difficult the first time. And how about celebrating when we do create those boundaries? Why don't we find a way to recognize that victory? My husband once took part in a ceremony in a larger Christian ministry context. The ceremony addressed unforgiveness in the participant's lives. They were instructed to write down the names of those they had never forgiven on a piece of dissolvable tissue paper. Then, those tiny pieces of paper were placed in water and disappeared as a testament to what forgiveness can look like. It was a way to recognize a small win in my husband's life. Maybe we can do the same? We could include many of the beliefs we have long held concerning our lives and values.

There are also those long-standing, very entrenched defense mechanisms we utilize when triggered by feelings from the past. I have used journaling for as long as I can remember to process my usage of those habitual mechanisms. Often, it is just a calendar that I carry around, but it gets filled with thoughts, ideas, and brainstorming for my life and what I want to do in a particular season. As I mentioned earlier in the book, practicing mindfulness techniques or strategies is the best way to help with those defense mechanisms. They have been lifesavers in my healing process.

Another difficult aspect of my journey has been to prioritize my needs and my pain. My husband will tell you I spend too much time and energy on his needs, neglecting my own. I am still working on this. One of the best ideas I have heard is for us to write a letter to our younger self. Grieving over that letter and providing hope, support, and comfort to myself at an earlier age allows me to feel more empowered to embrace self-care and focus on my needs here and now.

Another aspect of letter writing is that I can remind my inner child, my younger self, that the trauma I was exposed to was not my fault. I was too vulnerable to have prevented what happened. This has dramatically improved my willingness to look in the mirror and see value, self-esteem, and comfort. The letters are essential for reframing who I have seen myself as at other times.

Triggers that Rekindle Trauma

What about triggers? At this stage of my recovery, those trigger moments have become much like the story told in The Wizard of Oz. In my history, I did not have the tools to regulate my emotions, so those feelings were stored away behind emotional walls I built using defense mechanisms. As time went by, I would get triggered, not understanding that the trigger was not indicative of something happening at the moment. Instead, the trigger was a memory. What was happening in real-time reminded me of something in my past. This was an important lesson for me. When I began tearing down those emotional walls and processing the pain behind them, it was like Dorothy looking behind the curtain in The Wizard of Oz and seeing the regular man standing there with levers. He was not the wizard, after all. As I began tearing down those emotional walls, the triggers and subsequent memories that would surface were losing their power and influence over me. I realized that the impact of my emotional memory could be diminished as I processed the pain and abuse of my past.

My healing journey has frequently revolved around my need for forgiveness. Whether it was toward my stepfather or other abusers or if it was directed at myself, forgiveness has been a gift to me. By letting go of the toxic emotions tied to childhood trauma in my life, I have created a climate of emotional freedom and personal growth. Our trauma must not define our journey of healing. By embracing forgiveness, as survivors, we can reframe our past, pave the way for renewed relationships, and discover who we were designed to be.

Applying Self-Compassion and Self-Care

This leads us to the most critical aspect of maintaining a healing climate from our past. I am referring to self-compassion and self-care. They probably mean the same thing for some, but they are distinct within the therapeutic community. For me, self-compassion revolves around how I would treat a friend or a loved one going through a recovery process. What would I say to that person? How would I seek to encourage? What support might they need from me? In my situation, I took on many labels that were unhealthy for my growth and development. I spoke about these earlier in the chapter. I told myself from my youth that I wasn't worthy, lovable, and could not be trusted. This resulted from feeling a deep sense of shame early in life. So, what my inner circle and my husband have spent many years doing is to remind me of the value, worth, and importance I bring to their lives. This has made a massive difference in how I view myself. It has also been the impetus for reminding myself each day that I am worthy, I am lovable, I do matter, I can trust again, and I am important. This is the self-compassion I practice every day.

Self-care, however, is more of a practical application. This is how I live out my life daily, physically, intellectually, and spiritually. I am committed to beginning each day with quiet time for scripture reading, prayer, reflection, and meditation. I incorporate music as a therapy in preparation for the activities ahead during the day. These activities would include work, errands, etc. I also want to carve out time for exercise. This might consist of walking, calisthenics, or weightlifting. I want to do something that unleashes any stored energy or emotions. Finally, I am constantly regulating my diet. I have been a comfort food fan at certain times in my life, which is not a good thing. So, eating healthy food has become a priority of mine for most of my adult life. Finally, there are a few other activities that I have tried to incorporate as a holistic form of self-care/compassion. This list includes:

- Remember to continue setting boundaries in all relationships.

- Continue processing the pain of the past, either through self-help or therapy.

- Locating support groups either online or in person.

- Soaking up all the information on healing from reliable sources.

- Establishing good routines for daily activities, including proper rest.

- Incorporating fun activities that can be shared with family or friends.

- And constantly affirming my current self and my inner child.

Healing from Childhood trauma is a journey, one marked by challenges and the processing of many emotions. Nevertheless, as we reach the point of writing a new narrative for our lives, we step into a position of empowerment—a place where the pain and abuse of our past no longer dictate our future. This can be an opportunity to reclaim our voice, establish our true identity, and experience the beauty and joy of our transformation.

Writing this new narrative means we can choose healing over avoidance, compassion over self-criticism, and hope over despair. When we were children, we did not have control over the trauma we were exposed to. We were powerless. As adults, we now can choose. Each choice becomes like a stepping stone toward our new narrative. A narrative that better aligns with who we were designed to be. A narrative that coalesces with our values, dreams, and best self. What a beautiful setting to begin living a life of freedom from the past.

The Hope of Neuroplasticity

The results of writing a new narrative are multifaceted, as discussed in this chapter. However, the one area we have not discussed may be the most important: the concept of neuroplasticity. This refers to our brain's ability to reorganize itself by forming new neural connections in response to changes we make in recovery. This process allows the brain to adapt, recover, and grow throughout life. How does this work?

When we learn something new, neurons (brain cells) communicate by sending electrical signals across synapses (connections between neurons). The more frequently these pathways are used, the stronger and more efficient they become. A phrase in the neuroscience world says, "Neurons that fire together wire together." Essentially, the brain can begin storing new memories instead of the old ones. The therapeutic activities we embark on can encourage these healthy patterns of thought to replace those associated with the trauma of our past eventually. This is the most wonderful news of all.

In summary, neuroplasticity allows for growth, recovery, and transformation at any stage in life. This can provide the foundation for our new narrative. One that is aimed at the beauty and growth of our healing journey. This science of neuroplasticity validates what our hope has long suggested: healing is possible, and the brain is an extraordinary ally in our journey.

Key Takeaways

- The most important benefit of a support group or person may be that they can remind us of our value and worth.

- The key to unlearning emotional habits and breaking down emotional walls is grasping the concept of self-regulation.

- Setting healthy boundaries in our relationships is a way to ensure, amongst other things, that we promote our self-worth, build trust, reduce overdependence on others, and build authentic connections in those relationships.

- It is important to realize that the impact of our emotional memory is diminished as we process the pain and abuse of the past.

- Letting go of the emotions tied to our past can create a climate of emotional freedom and personal growth.

- Neuroplasticity allows growth, recovery, and transformation at any stage of life.

RESTORING THE BROKEN PIECES

Chapter 8 Journal

1. What are some of the most significant challenges you have faced, and how can you use those experiences to write a new narrative?

_____

_____

_____

_____

_____

_____

_____

_____

_____

_____

_____

_____

_____

_____

_____

_____

_____

_____

_____

_____

Chapter 8 Journal

2. What values are the most important to you, and how can they guide your life moving forward?

_____
_____
_____
_____
_____
_____
_____
_____
_____
_____
_____
_____
_____
_____
_____
_____
_____
_____
_____
_____
_____
_____

Chapter 8 Journal

3. Imagine your life one year from now, free from the burdens of your past. What are you doing? How does it feel in this new narrative?

_____
_____
_____
_____
_____
_____
_____
_____
_____
_____
_____
_____
_____
_____
_____
_____
_____
_____
_____

Chapter 8 Journal

4. What parts of your identity are you most proud of today? What new aspects do you want to cultivate in the future?

_____
_____
_____
_____
_____
_____
_____
_____
_____
_____
_____
_____
_____
_____
_____
_____
_____
_____

Chapter 8 Exercise

Letter to Your Younger Self:

Write a letter to your younger self, offering compassion, understanding, and encouragement. Acknowledge their pain but let them know how far you have come since.

Chapter 8 Worksheet

My New Narrative:

Section 1: Identify three key beliefs about yourself that are based on the pain and abuse of your past.

Section 2: Rewrite each of those key beliefs into a positive, empowering, and encouraging statement.

Section 3: Outline one practical step you can take to reinforce these key beliefs in your daily life.

Chapter 9

Sustaining Our Healing Journey

My husband and I were adult converts to Christianity. We had the same spiritual mentor during the early years of our newfound faith life. My husband shared a story about him years ago that has impacted me since. Our mentor said he had what he called a "pot of love" on the kitchen counter at home. He would write down affirmations on paper and place these in the pot every day. His reasoning was clear. He knew that even though he loved his wife and children, he would make mistakes daily that could hurt their feelings or create conflict. The affirmations reminded his family of the depth of his love and commitment to them.

We now come to the chapter "Sustaining Our Healing Journey." Here, we will learn how to identify sources of contention in our day-to-day lives, explore strategies to navigate the obstacles and challenges we face, and gain practical tools to help us stay the course of our new narrative. The story above should inspire us. It should remind us that even though we are on the road to recovery, there will be days when we do not measure up to our expectations of what a changed life looks like. We should be prepared to have our pot of love on the kitchen counter filled with reminders of how far we have come, how resilient we have been, and what our future looks like with our new narrative.

Sources of Contention

Since beginning a healing journey, I have seen patterns of contention in my life. These patterns of thinking and feeling can be traced to a few different ideas. The first is the primary obstacle I have faced in my years of recovery: triggers. Triggers have always transported me back to a place and time that was painful. It could be a sound, a smell, or a situation – but in every case, I was reminded of a memory. I have experienced this more frequently as I interacted with my family. So, what can we do about the triggers that seemingly come out of nowhere? What has been beneficial to me is to create a journal about those triggers once they pass. I have read other articles that call this a trigger log. Whatever we decide to call it, it is an invaluable tool. For me, this means asking myself what triggered the reaction, what emotion I experienced at that moment, whether there were any physical feelings, and whether I was able to respond with a helpful coping strategy; if not, how might I respond more effectively the next time I am in a similar situation.

A second obstacle for me has been what could be called external stressors. I struggled for a few years after beginning my healing journey with this type of obstacle. I had seen my life change, my thoughts renewed, especially with my newfound faith. So why was I still struggling? Many of us have this challenge. I was often feeling overworked and unable to find time to focus on recovery. As I write, I feel overwhelmed on some days at work. I should not, but the demands of my employer are occasionally unrealistic. In response, I want to see how to prioritize each aspect of my day-to-day activities to feel in control with a plan to address those stressors.

There are also demands on my emotional well-being that revolve around my home life, marriage, and finances. Each of these areas initiates a sense of worry. Here is where I have to be my best self. Otherwise, thoughts like self-doubt, fear, and the possibility of relying again on those old defense mechanisms quickly overtake my mind. The silver lining for me is that knowing these patterns of my past empowers me to respond quickly with the necessary steps to stay present in the moment, reminding me that life is often challenging and that I have come too far to look back now. I have nothing to fear; change should not be something to fear but rather a sign of progress.

Building Resilience to Face the Challenges

Years ago, I decided to run a marathon. I spent months training for this event. Although I had a training partner, she relied on me to equip us for the day we would run 26.2 miles. I did precisely that. I put together a running schedule to ensure we worked up to that distance and ran that distance before the event. We were prepared for our struggles on race day because we looked at the challenges before us. This applies to all of us trying to build greater levels of resilience to sustain our healing process. Resilience is the foundation for navigating the obstacles we face in recovery. It is not just about bouncing back from failure but more about adapting and growing stronger as we overcome each obstacle in our new narrative. So, how do we adapt and grow stronger? How do we heal?

Healing is hard. Some days, we will feel strong; other days, we may feel the opposite. Here is where self-compassion and self-care come in. If we had a friend in our situation, would we not reach out to encourage and provide kindness and consideration to them? Of course, we would. On those difficult days, we have to acknowledge the pain. We must be willing to say, "This is hard, but I am going to get through it." We need that pot of love on our kitchen counter with those written affirmations. We must avoid self-criticism during difficult moments, replace those thoughts with "healing takes time" and "look how much progress I have made." Remember how much those obstacles have helped you get to this day. Be prepared with many sticky notes plastered everywhere in your home that say, "Every challenge you are facing today is preparing you for future obstacles and success, as well." In other words, adopt a growth mindset. You are in recovery. You are growing. You are getting further away from your past. You are becoming more and more like your true self.

Embrace Your Setbacks

I elaborated on the stages of grief in Chapter 2. My husband and I could not come to terms with our feelings about our childhood trauma until we learned about the grieving process. Once we were able to understand why we were feeling the way we did, the ups and downs associated with our past trauma, as well as our current failures, began to make sense. I think we began to see that those feelings were not only expected but to be anticipated as well. The ideas from our Christian faith began to be incorporated. We both knew we could not be Christ's perfect imitations and that we would sometimes sin and fail. Thus, we could see failure in a different light. This is when we began seeing recovery along the same lines. We told ourselves that everyone in recovery has setbacks. What is important is how we respond to those setbacks.

A few more concepts began to unfold in our lives as we came to terms with our sometimes flawed or failed outcomes in recovery. These included, at least for me, the thought process of what I could have done differently in a failed experience. How could I have responded in an emotionally healthier way to that trigger? Did I see the repetition from a previous pattern of responses? The setbacks I have experienced in my healing journey have led me to rethink some of my earlier ideas about how to work out my recovery. Those setbacks have led me to incorporate yoga and music therapy to prepare myself more effectively for the journey ahead. We have to admit that setbacks are inevitable but also incredibly valuable. I have always learned more about myself, my work performance, my struggles, etc., through my mistakes, not my successes. Be encouraged that setbacks are opportunities for growth in our healing process.

Developing Your Team

I have co-sponsored marriage ministry programs with my husband over the past fifteen years. One of the popular workshops we provide discusses personality and temperament differences. Temperament theory can be traced to ancient Greek philosophers. Terms were coined in the second century to describe the four prominent personalities or temperaments. I am unquestionably a phlegmatic. I mention this because it represents my essential character traits. I am an introvert. This temperament type would be considered laid back, easygoing, and service-oriented. I would also find stability, energy, and comfort away from others instead of with people. So, being in a group context is extremely difficult, as is being open and honest about my feelings. The importance of building a support system is thus not intuitive to me. It is one of the hardest things I have ever done. Learning that being open and honest in a group setting was part of my life coach training consumed me with fear. Looking back, what Neecie, her team, and my fellow students did in support of my training was a crucial facet of my healing journey. I was forced to develop trust, come out of my introverted shell, and begin opening up about my childhood trauma.

As you continue your healing journey, it will be vital for you to develop your team of supporters. This can include family, friends, counselors or therapists, and group settings. The important thing is not to attempt self-help in isolation. The people around you must validate your experience and will be there to remind you of your worth and value and that you are not alone. This process can seem incredibly hard, especially if you are an introvert like me, and is compounded by difficulty when trust issues are at the core of our being. But it is so worth it.

Tools for the Endgame

I have often considered putting together a tool kit or a toolbox for my current grounding needs. A few years ago, I used a small treasure chest. What would go into such a box? How about something small you could put into your hands to feel it? Something could be scented as well. Scents significantly impact me, so having something I can smell nearby is essential. And, of course, the pot of love with affirmations and those sticky notes must be a priority for us as we prepare for any potential challenges.

Finally, why not create a timeline for our progress? One that allows us to see the level of resilience we continue to develop every day. My husband created the life map for his childhood trauma. We should also make one for our wins and growth and place it somewhere in our homes to be reminded daily of our continued resilience and stability.

Our journey will still have challenges, but we now have the tools and strength to face them. We must trust in our ability to continue growing. Remember that healing is not about avoiding the obstacles. Instead, overcoming every obstacle and challenge deepens our resilience and strengthens our healing. We are more than capable of creating a life now that honors our past while embracing our future. We have a new narrative. This is the most glorious part of our healing journey.

Key Takeaways

- Positive written affirmations should be part of a healing journey. Placing them in our homes, cars, and workplaces reminds us of our continued recovery.

- Creating a trigger journal or log provides a way to track our progress, discover what constantly trips us up, and remind us of what we need to prepare for.

- Self-criticism must be avoided to facilitate growth and stability.

- Embracing setbacks takes the fear out of them and allows us to view them through a different perspective – as opportunities to learn from.

- We should strive to surround ourselves with a steady stream of supporters and encouragers. We need people in our lives who validate our healing process.

- Create a trigger toolbox that holds items you can touch, smell, and see as a grounding exercise when we are triggered.

Chapter 9 Journal

1. Reflect on a recent challenge you faced. What emotions did it evoke? How did you respond, and what did you learn from the experience?

_____
_____
_____
_____
_____
_____
_____
_____
_____
_____
_____
_____
_____
_____
_____
_____
_____
_____
_____
_____
_____
_____
_____

Chapter 9 Journal

2. Think about three moments in your healing journey that made you proud. What did they prove about your true self?

_____
_____
_____
_____
_____
_____
_____
_____
_____
_____
_____
_____
_____
_____
_____
_____
_____
_____
_____
_____

Chapter 9 Journal

3. Ask yourself: Why is healing important to me? What changes do I hope to see as I continue this journey?

Chapter 9 Journal

4. Envision your healed self. Describe in detail what your life would look and feel like. What small actions today can bring you closer to that vision?

_____

_____

_____

_____

_____

_____

_____

_____

_____

_____

_____

_____

_____

_____

_____

_____

_____

_____

_____

_____

_____

Chapter 9 Exercise

The Resilience Ritual:

Purpose: Create a consistent practice to affirm your healing progress.

Step-by-Step:

- Choose a consistent time each week to have a session.

- Pick a quiet spot in your home for quiet time. Use soft meditation music and/or candles to induce a sense of serenity.

- Pick out a journal prompt from the book to work on.

- Spend 10-15 minutes meditating on your answer. Try to focus on being calm and feeling safe.

- Finally, end with a moment of thankfulness for where you are now and where you are heading in your healing journey.

Chapter 9 Worksheet

Trigger Reflection Worksheet:

Purpose: A tool to help us understand and process our triggers.

Section	Your Response
Trigger	Describe the situation or event that triggered you.
Emotion(s) Felt	Identify the emotions that came up (e.g., fear, sadness, anger).
Physical Response	Note any physical reactions (e.g., tight chest, trembling).
What It Reminds Me Of	Reflect on any memories or past events it brought to mind.
Coping Strategy Used	Detail how you managed the trigger in the moment.
What I Learned	Write down one thing you learned about yourself or your process from this event.

Chapter 10

Healing the Wounds of Complex Trauma

The final destination for our exploration of healing from childhood trauma takes us to complex post-traumatic stress disorder, or CPTSD for short. CPTSD is, by definition, a psychological condition that arises from prolonged and repeated trauma. In my case, it was due to the impact that both sexual abuse and domestic violence had on my childhood. While PTSD is commonly associated with childhood abuse, it is also attributed to singular events. Not so for CPTSD, which reflects the cumulative effect of ongoing abuse or neglect. CPTSD not only impacts how individuals like me process trauma but also profoundly shapes my sense of self and my relationships. This chapter will explore CPTSD, its effects on daily life, and how individuals can find hope and healing. Recognizing CPTSD is essential to understanding the profound ways trauma can shape a person—and how recovery is possible with the right tools and support.

Describing and Manifesting CPTSD

Therapists believe that the roots of CPTSD can be traced back to childhood when individuals like me endured multiple forms of adverse childhood experiences. It was during those early years of life that my caregivers failed to provide the basic needs I had for emotional and physical well-being. When the sexual abuse I was exposed to is combined with the ongoing domestic violence that was in our home, each of the experiences tends to compound the previous ones. This creates a pervasive sense of helplessness and hopelessness. The symptoms of CPTSD include emotional dysregulation, changes in behavior such as avoidance, and relational challenges due to the lack of trust in the home.

The Impact of CPTSD

The emotional and psychological impact that CPTSD left on me was manifested in multiple ways. I grew into adolescence and adulthood with a deep sense of shame and unworthiness.

This underlying framework of my inner self only induced cycles of depression, anxiety, and self-blame for my failures. I had a heightened sense of fear, which always made it difficult for me to feel safe. I must admit that this has been a lifelong struggle – feeling secure in my circumstances.

I would agree with therapists who say that the impact of CPTSD is not only on our minds but also includes an imprint on our physical bodies. According to experts in the field, CPTSD clients may experience chronic pain, digestive issues, or other unexplained physical symptoms (Van Der Kolk, 2014). Neurologically, the amygdala (responsible for the fight-or-flight-or-freeze-or-fawn response) may become overactive, while the prefrontal cortex, which governs rational thinking, may underperform. This, at first glance, is quite scary. Additionally, CPTSD can make forming and maintaining healthy relationships difficult. Patterns of toxic relationships may emerge as individuals subconsciously recreate the dynamics of past abuse.

Conversely, some may isolate themselves entirely, fearing vulnerability and rejection. This would describe my life as a teen and into early adulthood. This would also be where I kept hearing Nadine's words about cycles of abuse being generational but that I could end such in my recovery.

Healing from CPTSD

CPTSD is highly complex, so the healing process often requires professional support. I have learned that trauma-focused therapies like Eye Movement Desensitization and Reprocessing (EMDR) and Cognitive Behavioral Therapy (CBT) can help individuals reprocess traumatic memories more effectively. In my case, the healing would result from CBT and Cognitive Processing Therapy (CPT) exposure. It is recommended that those who have been diagnosed with CPTSD also find a group to plug into. This provides a sense of connection, and the shared experience can provide hope. Being isolated can prove detrimental to our healing of this complex condition.

The healing process, at least from a self-help perspective, is the same as discussed throughout this book. We must begin exploring our thought processes through journaling and learn to self-regulate through the many strategies discussed earlier. We need to manage triggers to assist us during those flashback moments. We must reframe our self-worth and self-image through the self-compassion and self-care methods we discussed. How else can we begin to change the negative images about ourselves and begin instead to have a sense of worthiness and value?

The final healing phase involves creating a life of safety, purpose, and joy. This means establishing healthy boundaries, nurturing supportive and reciprocal relationships, and finding purpose for the pain in our lives. Small wins should be celebrated as milestones in a journey that is as much about rediscovering oneself as overcoming the past. Many of us only discover our true selves once we have reached this state.

I know that the discussion above is quite daunting. I am here to say, though, that healing is not only possible but necessary if you have experienced, like me, multiple forms of abuse in your past. If you were to ask my friends and co-workers, they would likely say they never knew I had struggled for many years with the symptoms associated with CPTSD. But I have. The effects of CPTSD feel isolating, but you need to know that many others share your life experience. Whether it is through therapy, support groups, or connecting with loved ones and friends, seeking out safe and supportive relationships can be transformative as we wrestle with the pain and abuse of our past. Here is where I get adamant about finding purpose for the pain in our lives. Sharing our story can be the catalyst of change in the lives of others who, too, suffer from childhood trauma.

Finally, we must envision the life we want to create beyond the trauma. While CPTSD may have shaped parts of our past, it does not have to dictate our future. The work we are doing now—to understand, process, and heal—lays the foundation for a life filled with meaning, joy, and connection. Let's restore those broken pieces.

Key Takeaways

- Complex post-traumatic stress disorder (CPTSD) is a psychological condition that arises from prolonged and repeated trauma.

- CPTSD profoundly shapes how one views a sense of self and relationships.

- CPTSD impacts a person's mind and leaves an imprint on the physical body.

- Neurologically, the amygdala may become overactive, while the prefrontal cortex may underperform in the person diagnosed with CPTSD.

- Because healing from CPTSD can be highly complex, therapy is often recommended.

- Finding help in support groups can provide context and support for those diagnosed with CPTSD.

Chapter 10 Journal

1. What does a sense of safety mean to you? Describe a time or place where you felt completely safe. How can you incorporate more of that feeling into your life right now?

Chapter 10 Journal

2. Reflect on a recurring emotion or thought from your past trauma. When did you first notice it, and how has it shaped your self-perception?

Chapter 10 Journal

3. Write about a situation where you felt triggered recently. What emotions, thoughts, or physical sensations did you experience? How did you respond?

Chapter 10 Journal

4. Reflect on a relationship in your life. How has your experience with CPTSD influenced your interactions with this person? What steps could you take to improve trust or communication?

_____
_____
_____
_____
_____
_____
_____
_____
_____
_____
_____
_____
_____
_____
_____
_____
_____
_____
_____

Chapter 10 Exercise

Grounding Through Sensory Awareness:

Purpose: To help manage emotional overwhelm and bring focus to the present moment.

Instructions:
- Sit in a quiet space and focus on your breathing.
- Identify:
    - 5 things you can see,
    - 4 things you can touch,
    - 3 things you can hear,
    - 2 things you can smell, and
    - 1 thing you can taste.
- Write about how this exercise made you feel and note any differences in your emotional state afterward.

Chapter 10 Worksheet

Reframing Negative Beliefs:

Purpose: To challenge and reframe limiting beliefs rooted in trauma.

Instructions:

- Write down negative beliefs you hold about yourself (e.g., "I am unlovable").
- Identify the origin of each belief. Where do you think it came from?
- Reframe each belief into a positive, empowering statement (e.g., "I am worthy of love and connection").
- Use the space provided to write a journal about how adopting these new beliefs could impact your healing journey.

Negative Belief:	**Origin**	Reframed Belief:
Example: "I can't trust anyone."	**Childhood neglect**	"I am learning to trust safe, supportive people."

Conclusion

As we come to the close of *Restoring the Broken Pieces: Healing from Childhood Trauma*, I want to pause and reflect on our journey together. I did not write this book to be a memoir or just a simple guide to healing from the pain and abuse of the past. Instead, I wrote it as an invitation to those who may never have understood the "why" of their past and the "how" to move forward. To undertake the healing journey from childhood trauma is a profound act of courage. It requires facing part of ourselves that has always felt broken and far too painful to examine.

In this book, we have discovered many aspects of the healing journey. We have found out what childhood trauma is and how it lingers into adulthood when we do not address it in a therapeutic context. We have explored how trauma leaves an imprint that is often invisible to others but is manifested in relationships with them. Plus how trauma can lead to anxiety, depression, trust issues, etc.

We have also discovered the concept of the inner child within us - that tender, vulnerable part that carries the wounds of our past. Reconnecting with our inner child has given us insight into the importance of self-compassion and how providing this to ourselves can transform internal blame, shame, and guilt into encouragement and affirmation. A relationship with our inner child is about healing the past and nurturing a foundation for rebuilding a new life that guides our recovery process.

Triggers were also explored, the most challenging aspect of my healing journey. We learned how they can activate old memories, pulling us back to those moments of pain and abuse and away from our present state. We discovered the tools needed to help us navigate these triggers and give us a sense of control over the feelings that surface when we are triggered. Those are the feelings we never understood. They seemingly came out of nowhere and disrupted our day-to-day. We can now respond with greater awareness, strength, and understanding.

For me, the power of forgiveness has taken on new meaning. I struggled for many years with unforgiveness, thinking that excusing or forgetting defined true forgiveness. Nothing could be further from the truth. Instead, true forgiveness is about releasing the weight of our bitterness, regret, and anger so we can move forward without those who violated us still having control over our lives.

Throughout the book, I have emphasized the importance and value of having a support group or person in place during this healing journey. This would include both personally and professionally when you are able. The reason is simple. Trauma is not something we are meant to face alone. The personal relationship(s) give us the love and connection we desperately want and need to feel whole. My husband has made a difference in my recovery as a sounding board and source of encouragement, and seeking professional support can provide a structured and safe environment for our healing journey.

We must never forget that healing is not a linear process. I have had days in my journey when I felt empowered and free from the past. There have also been days when I felt like I had taken steps back. What I have come to learn is that this is normal. Every setback has become an opportunity for me to understand my past better. This has led to a more precise definition of my true self and a more thorough reframing of my past. One that has allowed me to unpack the pain, confront it, and ensure it loses its hold on my life.

As you continue your journey, I encourage you to monitor your progress closely. Healing cannot be just about surviving anymore. We must see it as an opportunity to thrive. We must see it as an opportunity to rebuild our lives, find peace and resilience, and discover the connections and relationships we have felt out of reach for so long. Plus, the healing on your journey will ensure you find meaning and purpose for the days ahead.

I want to say to the person holding this book: I see you and your pain but also your hope and strength. The broken pieces of your past are worth saving. You are not defined by what happened to you but by how you choose to respond moving forward. Thank you for allowing me to be part of your journey. Writing this book has been an act of healing for me as well. I am deeply honored to share in our healing together. May we always remember that trauma can wound us, but it cannot destroy our potential. As you continue your journey, may you carry the lessons and tools from this book, using them to build a new narrative, one that is filled with peace and hope.

You are not alone.

With all my heart,

Melissa Alvis

Appendix

Self-Help Guides for Healing and Growth

This appendix is designed as a practical resource for complementing the chapters in the book. *Restoring the Broken Pieces: Healing from Childhood Trauma* has been created to allow readers to come alongside my personal story while learning the foundational principles to forge their healing journey. The worksheets within the appendix are quick-start tools for better understanding the healing process. I hope these guides will provide straightforward information that can assist all readers in their quest to remain grounded, process their emotions, and navigate their recovery process moving forward.

Each guide addresses a unique aspect of the healing process, ensuring you have a reference when needed. Whether you are just starting your recovery or have been on your journey for a while, I hope you can turn here during those moments of uncertainty or struggle.

- **Appendix A** offers an outline of the struggles we face as survivors of childhood trauma and what the ramifications are entering adulthood. My personal story includes these points, so I have tried to offer up what I know has worked in my life or the life of my inner circle.

- **Appendix B** focuses on the steps needed when faced with trauma triggers from the past. We are reminded that triggers are memories from the past and not current events. Thus, we need to know how to respond when they arise.

- **Appendix C** explores what it means to do inner child work. This was overlooked in my self-help process early on but has become extremely important as I discover more areas of my past in need of healing.

- **Appendix D** highlights the primary aspects of entering into a self-help healing journey. Here, I will outline the talking points that need to be the focus of a recovery process, especially one meant for self-discovery strategies.

I hope these pages provide quick access to the reader and are practical in their application. Having tools in the moment of need is important as we walk through the pain and abuse of our past. May you be empowered with knowledge and strategies that remind you that healing is possible and that you are never alone.

Appendix A

Struggles Faced by Adults Healing from Childhood Trauma

- **Feelings of Shame and Guilt:** As survivors, we are often left with the residue of feeling we were responsible for the trauma. The goal is to understand that we are not to blame and use self-compassion to address the negative self-talk and self-perception.

- **Inability to Trust Others:** Abuse and betrayal leave an imprint that others are not to be trusted. Instead of constantly fearing being hurt, we must seek to build safe relationships and discern whom we should and should not trust.

- **Emotional Dysregulation:** Many of us struggle in the management of intense emotions such as anxiety or sadness. We must use strategies that help us self-regulate to express feelings more effectively.

- **Low Self-Esteem:** As survivors, we often feel unworthy of love or happiness, which often leads to avoidance. Instead, we need to begin working on those affirmations and sticky notes. Doing so cultivates feelings of self-love, acceptance, and self-respect.

- **Triggers and Flashbacks:** Triggers remind us of trauma memory, while flashbacks seem to place us in the middle of the memory of the event. Either way, the feelings are fearful. We need to manage the impact of these struggles by practicing mindfulness techniques (triggers) and developing grounding techniques (flashbacks).

- **Misplaced Boundaries:** Many survivors still struggle with establishing healthy boundaries with others. This could lead to us becoming people-pleasers, overcommitting ourselves, and even seeing others violate our personal space or needs. We have to learn how to establish boundaries and to say no.

- **Relational Pitfalls:** Trauma leads to a fear of intimacy, difficulties with trust, and even repeating toxic patterns from the past. We must learn how to connect with others healthily.

- **Avoidance:** We tend to numb emotional pain with substance use, work, food, etc. Instead, we should seek support and develop healthy coping mechanisms.

- **Unresolved Anger:** Unexpressed anger from past trauma can develop into feelings of frustration or even rage. We must learn creative and healthy ways to process anger and seek to understand the underlying cause.

- **Find Meaning and Purpose:** Trauma leads us to disconnect from our true selves, our passions, our goals, etc. We must explore who we are and what we want in life to move past the haunting shadows of our past.

Appendix B

Steps for Managing Trauma Triggers

- **Recognize the Trigger:** Try to understand the source of the trigger. Recognizing the trigger will help us not to react so strongly moving forward. Plus, it reminds us that this is only a memory, not something happening now.

- **Stop and Breathe:** Stop and breathe. Take a moment and try one of the breathing exercises. Deep breathing helps activate the parasympathetic nervous system, which calms the body's fight-or-flight-or-freeze-or-fawn response.

- **Get Grounded:** Use Grounding Techniques that help bring us back to the here and now. The common one is the five things we can see, four things we can touch, three things we can hear, two things we can smell, and one thing we can taste. This interrupts the trigger.

- **Feel the Moment:** Allow yourself to feel valid emotions. This helps us reassure ourselves that we are not going crazy but only having a memory crop up—a painful memory, for sure, but not anything in the present.

- **Reframe the Moment:** We must remind ourselves that this is not a current event. That allows us to separate the painful past from the present.

- **Calm the Waters:** Try soothing instruments like aromas or music. This creates a sense of comfort and safety as we are brought to a calm place.

- **Practice Meditation:** Use meditation to allow yourself to stay in the present. Focus on your breathing and allow the intensity of the trigger to pass by.

- **Reach out for Support:** In the moment, reach out to a trusted family member or friend as a supporter. Try to talk through the feelings. Being isolated is the worst thing we can do in those moments.

- **Challenge Negative Thoughts:** Resist negative self-talk. Identify negative thoughts and challenge them with affirmations or reframed ideas.

- **Exercise:** Work out. Try to get out and walk or do other exercises to release those pent-up emotions. Physical activity releases endorphins, which improve our mood.

- **Find a Safe Place:** Create a safe place at home, a retreat if you will, where you can go and feel safe and comfortable. This could be a favorite place to sit, a quiet room that allows you to be at ease.

- **Reflect and Process:** Finally, after the storm of the trigger has passed, try to reflect on what happened, how you felt, and what you tried to do in the moment to ease the burden. Learn from what just happened.

Appendix C

Healing Our Inner Child

Please note that even though inner child work can provide healing at the deepest level, it should be done with a trusted friend/family member or, better yet, a trusted counselor or therapist. We all need to do inner child work in a safe and supportive environment. We are survivors of childhood trauma and need to process the emotions we have carried since. We also need to understand patterns of thought and behavior. Professional support tools are important and allow for more effective and transformative healing. With that said, here are some self-help steps for healing:

- **Acknowledge Your Inner Child:** Simply recognize that our inner child holds wounds from our childhood trauma experiences.

- **Design a Safe Place to Heal:** Find a quiet place where you can feel safe, providing a reflective and calming environment.

- **Know Your Triggers:** At the outset, list the known triggers that have affected you, internal (fear, anger, etc.) and external (sights and sounds).

- **Have Grounding Techniques:** Know how to use grounding techniques, meditation, or breathing exercises to stay in the present.

- **Find a Safe Place to Visualize:** Once in your safe place, visualize your younger self. What age are they? What is their expression? What are they saying?

- **Connect with Your Inner Child:** Try to dialogue with your inner child. Speak with compassion, empathy, and kindness as the parent you wish you had.

- **Identify Those Negative Thoughts:** Identify any negative self-talk your younger self engages in and respond with affirmations, helping them set boundaries and offering encouragement.

- **Prepare to Feel:** Allow yourself to wade through the clutter of emotions your inner child may exhibit.

- **Offer Up Forgiveness:** Determine how to offer forgiveness to those responsible for the trauma.

- **Journal the Experience:** Allow yourself to journal the experience and write a letter to your younger self expressing the self-compassion you needed then but can provide now.

- **Seek Professional Support:** We must seek professional support to ensure a stable and safe therapeutic environment.

Appendix D

Fundamentals of a Self-Help Journey

It is vitally important for anyone beginning a healing journey to focus on specific aspects of the recovery process that relate to motivation and commitment. Healing from childhood trauma can be a long and challenging endeavor that requires persistence and resilience. The following practices lay a framework for lasting growth and true transformation:

- **Clarity of the Healing Process:** We must understand why healing is necessary and what goals must be set.

- **A Support System:** We need others who can come alongside to encourage and keep us grounded. The need for a support group works for some, while others may also need professional help.

- **Self-Compassion:** We have to be okay with making mistakes. We must give ourselves grace and focus on what we are getting right, not wrong.

- **Celebrate Small Wins:** We could keep a journal or hang something on the wall that gives us visibility of all our victories as we pursue healing.

- **A Growth Mindset:** Challenges are to be considered growth opportunities. We must believe that healing and transformation are not only possible but probable as we put in the work.

- **Consistent Routines:** We must establish a structured approach to our journey and develop daily habits that lead to consistent transformation.

- **Accountability:** Being honest and open about our struggles frees us from trying to be perfect. It also allows us to normalize the way our healing journey is unfolding. It ensures that when we have someone in our corner, we will receive feedback and accountability from their input. And trust them with our vulnerabilities.

- **We Must Be Grateful:** This is about seeing the glass half-full instead of half-empty. It is a daily practice of being thankful for second chances and the opportunity to write a new narrative.

- **Getting Plenty of Rest:** We need to remember how much emotional energy we draw from each day and be diligent about getting rest.

- **Get Educated:** Many resources are available to assist us in recovery. Whether that is books, videos, classes, etc., there are many avenues to learning and understanding every aspect of childhood trauma.

- **Faith or a Spiritual Connection:** My faith equipped me for the healing journey I began many years ago. Faith provided purpose and meaning to my life, allowing me to rise above the obstacles of my past.

- **A Vision Statement:** Writing down goals gives them life. So, believe in your dreams.

Glossary of Terms

A

- **Adverse Childhood Experiences (ACEs):** Traumatic events occurring before age 18, such as abuse, neglect, or household dysfunction, which can have long-term impacts on health and well-being.

- **Attachment Theory:** A psychological model describing how early relationships with caregivers influence emotional bonds and relationships in adulthood.

B

- **Breathwork:** Controlled breathing exercises designed to reduce stress, promote relaxation, and improve emotional regulation.

C

- **Cognitive Behavioral Therapy (CBT):** A structured, short-term psychotherapy that identifies and changes negative thought patterns and behaviors.

- **Cognitive Processing Therapy (CPT):** A specific type of CBT tailored for trauma survivors to address and reframe trauma-related thoughts.

- **Complex Trauma:** Repeated or prolonged exposure to traumatic events, often interpersonal in nature, such as abuse or neglect.

- **Co-Regulation:** The process by which one person's calm, regulated state helps another achieve emotional equilibrium.

- **Coping Mechanisms:** Strategies used to manage stress, or trauma that can be adaptive (helpful) or maladaptive (harmful).

D

- **Dialectical Behavior Therapy (DBT):** Combining cognitive-behavioral techniques with mindfulness to improve emotional regulation and interpersonal skills.

- **Dissociation:** A mental process where an individual disconnects from thoughts, feelings, or memories as a response to trauma.

E

- **Emotion Regulation:** The ability to manage and respond to emotional experiences healthily.

- **EMDR (Eye Movement Desensitization and Reprocessing):** A psychotherapy method using bilateral stimulation to help process and integrate traumatic memories.

F

- **Forgiveness:** The conscious decision to release feelings of resentment or vengeance toward those who have caused harm, facilitating emotional healing.

- **Fight, Flight, Freeze, or Fawn Response:** The body's automatic reactions to perceived threats are linked to the nervous system's response to trauma.

H

- **Hypervigilance:** A heightened state of awareness often experienced by trauma survivors, leading to a constant sense of threat or danger.

I

- **Inner Child:** The part of the psyche that retains the emotions, memories, and experiences of childhood, often central to trauma healing.

- **Internal Family Systems Therapy (IFS):** A therapeutic approach that views the mind as composed of distinct "parts" that can be healed and harmonized.

M

- **Mindfulness:** A practice of focusing on the present moment with non-judgmental awareness, often used to reduce anxiety and improve well-being.

N

- **Narrative Exposure Therapy (NET):** A therapy that helps individuals reconstruct their life stories to process traumatic events within a coherent narrative.

- **Neuroplasticity:** The brain's ability to adapt and form new neural connections in response to experiences is crucial for healing from trauma.

P

- **Post-Traumatic Growth (PTG):** Positive psychological changes that can occur as a result of struggling with trauma.

- **Prolonged Exposure Therapy (PE):** A structured therapy involving repeated exposure to trauma-related stimuli to reduce emotional distress over time.

R

- **Reframing:** A cognitive strategy to reinterpret negative thoughts or situations in a more positive or neutral light.
- **Resilience:** The ability to recover and adapt in adversity or trauma.

S

- **Self-Compassion:** Extending kindness and understanding to oneself, particularly in moments of failure or suffering.
- **Self-Regulation:** The ability to manage emotions, behaviors, and thoughts in challenging situations.
- **Somatic Therapy:** A body-centered therapy focusing on releasing stored trauma through bodily awareness and movement.
- **Sympathetic Nervous System (SNS):** The part of the autonomic nervous system that activates the "fight or flight" response.

T

- **Trauma-Informed Care:** This approach recognizes the widespread impact of trauma and prioritizes safety and empowerment in treatment.
- **Trauma Triggers:** Stimuli that evoke memories or responses related to past trauma.

References

General References on Childhood Trauma

- American Psychological Association. (n.d.). *What is a traumatic event?* Retrieved from https://www.apa.org.

- Felitti, V. J., Anda, R. F., Nordenberg, D., Williamson, D. F., Spitz, A. M., Edwards, V., & Marks, J. S. (1998). Relationship of childhood abuse and household dysfunction to many of the leading causes of death in adults: The Adverse Childhood Experiences (ACE) study. *American Journal of Preventive Medicine, 14*(4), 245–258.

- Lippard, E. T. C., & Nemeroff, C. B. (2019). The devastating clinical consequences of child abuse and neglect: Increased disease vulnerability and poor treatment response in mood disorders. *The American Journal of Psychiatry, 177*(1), 20–36.

- Van der Kolk, B. A. (2014). *The body keeps the score: Brain, mind, and body in the healing of trauma.* New York, NY: Viking.

Foundational Texts on Treatment Modalities for Childhood Trauma

- Briere, J., & Scott, C. (2015). *Principles of trauma therapy: A guide to symptoms, evaluation, and treatment* (2nd ed.). Thousand Oaks, CA: SAGE Publications.

- Cohen, J. A., Mannarino, A. P., & Deblinger, E. (2017). *Treating trauma and traumatic grief in children and adolescents* (2nd ed.). The Guilford Press.

- Courtois, C. A., & Ford, J. D. (2009). *Treating complex traumatic stress disorders: An evidence-based guide.* New York, NY: Guilford Press.

- Foa, E. B., Hembree, E. A., & Rothbaum, B. O. (2007). *Prolonged exposure therapy for PTSD: Emotional processing of traumatic experiences.* New York, NY: Oxford University Press.

- Greenberger, D., & Padesky, C. A. (2016). *Mind over mood: Change how you feel by changing the way you think* (2nd ed.). The Guilford Press.

- Herman, J. L. (1997). *Trauma and recovery: The aftermath of violence—From domestic abuse to political terror.* New York, NY: Basic Books.

- Levine, P. A. (1997). *Waking the tiger: Healing trauma.* North Atlantic Books.

- Linehan, M. M. (2014). *DBT skills training manual* (2nd ed.). New York, NY: Guilford Press.

- Resick, P. A., Monson, C. M., & Chard, K. M. (2016). *Cognitive processing therapy for PTSD: A comprehensive manual.* The Guilford Press.

- Schauer, M., Neuner, F., & Elbert, T. (2011). *Narrative exposure therapy: A short-term treatment for traumatic stress disorders.* Hogrefe Publishing.

- Schwartz, R. C., & Sweezy, M. (2020). *Internal family systems therapy* (2nd ed.). The Guilford Press.

- Shapiro, F. (2001). *Eye movement desensitization and reprocessing (EMDR): Basic principles, protocols, and procedures.* New York, NY: Guilford Press.

- Van der Kolk, B. A. (2002). Posttraumatic therapy in the age of neuroscience. *Psychoanalytic Dialogues, 12*(3), 381–392.

- Walker, P. (2013). *Complex PTSD: From surviving to thriving.* Lafayette, CA: Azure Coyote.

Books on Neuroplasticity

- Begley, S. (2009). *Train your mind, change your brain: How a new science reveals our extraordinary potential to transform ourselves.* New York, NY: Ballantine Books

- Doidge, N. (2007). *The brain that changes itself: Stories of personal triumph from the frontiers of brain science.* New York, NY: Viking.

- Doidge, N. (2015). *The brain's way of healing: Remarkable discoveries and recoveries from the frontiers of neuroplasticity.* New York, NY: Viking.

Books on the Concept of the Inner Child

- Bradshaw, J. (1990). *Homecoming: Reclaiming and championing your inner child.* New York, NY: Bantam Books.

- Miller, A. (1990). *The drama of the gifted child: The search for the true self.* New York, NY: Basic Books.

- Whitfield, C. L. (1987). *Healing the child within: Discovery and recovery for adult children of dysfunctional families.* Deerfield Beach, FL: Health Communications.

Books on Forgiveness

- Enright, R. D. (2001). *Forgiveness is a choice: A step-by-step process for resolving anger and restoring hope.* Washington, DC: American Psychological Association.

- Luskin, F. (2002). *Forgive for good: A proven prescription for health and happiness.* San Francisco, CA: HarperOne.

- Tutu, D., & Tutu, M. (2014). *The book of forgiving: The fourfold path for healing ourselves and our world.* San Francisco, CA: HarperOne.

Additional Foundational Works for Context

- Ainsworth, M. D. S., Blehar, M. C., Waters, E., & Wall, S. (1978). *Patterns of attachment: A psychological study of the strange situation.* Hillsdale, NJ: Erlbaum.

- Bowlby, J. (1969). *Attachment and loss: Vol. 1. Attachment.* New York, NY: Basic Books.

- Erikson, E. H. (1950). *Childhood and society.* New York, NY: Norton.

- Kübler-Ross, E. (1969). *On death and dying.* New York, NY: Macmillan.

- Liotti, G., & Farina, B. (2016). *Attachment in psychotherapy.* New York, NY: Routledge.

- MacLean, P. D. (1990). *The triune brain in evolution: Role in paleocerebral functions.* New York, NY: Springer.

The Power of Reflection: Journal Prompts for Healing

Journaling is one of the most powerful tools in our healing journey. We can discover more of ourselves as we share what is in our hearts and minds on paper. Writing can be a safe place to express what we think and feel.

I ensured journal prompts were associated with each chapter and its contents throughout the book. However, many other questions remain as we continue our recovery process. In this book's final section, I have included a series of additional prompts for you, my fellow travelers, to write about. I hope the following pages allow you to dive deeper into other aspects of your journey.

Remember the power of your words. In the past, they may have produced fear or pain. In the present, they can empower. Writing serves as a buffer between you and the past, between you and the negative self-talk, and between you and your future.

I hope the journal prompts throughout the book serve as a bridge between who you once were and who you are now becoming.

You are amazing!

Journal Prompts

1. What is one challenge you have overcome that you never thought you could? Could you explain how you did it?

_____
_____
_____
_____
_____
_____
_____
_____
_____
_____
_____
_____
_____
_____
_____
_____
_____
_____

Journal Prompts

2. Describe a place where you feel completely safe and at peace. What do you think makes it feel that way?

Journal Prompts

3. Who will you be when you get beyond your healing journey? What traits will describe you at that point?

_____
_____
_____
_____
_____
_____
_____
_____
_____
_____
_____
_____
_____
_____
_____
_____
_____
_____
_____

Journal Prompts

4. Since starting your journey, how have you changed or grown thus far?

___

Journal Prompts

5. Write about a small win you recently had in your life. How did it make you feel?

Journal Prompts

6. What is one negative belief you have about yourself? And how can you reframe with positive affirmations moving forward?

_____
_____
_____
_____
_____
_____
_____
_____
_____
_____
_____
_____
_____
_____
_____
_____
_____
_____
_____
_____

Journal Prompts

7. What techniques or tools have helped you the most in times of distress?

Journal Prompts

8. What does a fully healed you look like one day? Describe what healing would provide for you.

Journal Prompts

9. Write about a recent setback. How do you think you can use it to empower you moving forward?

Journal Prompts

10. List 5 things you are grateful for today. How do they bring you comfort, encouragement, or joy?

Journal Prompts

11. If you could speak to your younger self, what would you say to comfort and encourage them right now?

Journal Prompts

12. Is there someone you have been struggling to forgive? What would it look like to forgive them and how would that make you feel?

Journal Prompts

13. Identify a trigger that you experience most often. What can you do to remain grounded the next time you sense it?

_____
_____
_____
_____
_____
_____
_____
_____
_____
_____
_____
_____
_____
_____
_____
_____
_____
_____
_____
_____

Journal Prompts

14. Who do you currently have in your life as a supporter of your healing journey? How do they make a difference for you?

Journal Prompts

15. Write three affirmations you can repeat to yourself when you feel overwhelmed or discouraged.

_____
_____
_____
_____
_____
_____
_____
_____
_____
_____
_____
_____
_____
_____
_____
_____
_____
_____
_____
_____
_____

Journal Prompts

16. How would you show compassion to a friend going through a similar situation as yours?

Journal Prompts

17. What is the one thing you want to let go from your past more than any other?

Journal Prompts

18. What are the hopes you have for the next month, the next year? And what are you doing now to work towards those?

Journal Prompts

19. What does the idea of self-worth mean to you? Write about a time when you felt worthy.

Journal Prompts

20. Reflect on the time when you listened to your gut and made a decision of any consequence.

Journal Prompts

21. Have you ever had a moment when you found your voice? When you were able to speak, or able to set boundaries?

_____
_____
_____
_____
_____
_____
_____
_____
_____
_____
_____
_____
_____
_____
_____
_____
_____
_____
_____
_____

Journal Prompts

22. What boundaries do you need to set in your life right now? How can you implement them while remaining in a state of peace?

_____
_____
_____
_____
_____
_____
_____
_____
_____
_____
_____
_____
_____
_____
_____
_____
_____
_____

Journal Prompts

23. What is the one thing you are most ashamed of? How can you best separate what you are ashamed of from your personhood? Can you forgive yourself?

_____
_____
_____
_____
_____
_____
_____
_____
_____
_____
_____
_____
_____
_____
_____
_____
_____
_____
_____
_____

Journal Prompts

24. Write about the lessons your trauma has taught you. Do you think you can find a purpose for your pain?

_____
_____
_____
_____
_____
_____
_____
_____
_____
_____
_____
_____
_____
_____
_____
_____
_____
_____
_____
_____

Journal Prompts

25. Write a letter to yourself as if you are now healed. What would you say concerning the journey you have experienced?

_____
_____
_____
_____
_____
_____
_____
_____
_____
_____
_____
_____
_____
_____
_____
_____
_____
_____
_____
_____
_____
_____
_____

Journal Prompts

26. What one fear seems to be holding you back along your journey of healing? How can you gently face it and let go of its power?

Journal Prompts

27. What changes can you make in your living environment that would support your recovery process?

Journal Prompts

28. What activities, people, or places bring you joy and peace? How can you make more time for this in your life?

_____
_____
_____
_____
_____
_____
_____
_____
_____
_____
_____
_____
_____
_____
_____
_____
_____
_____
_____

Journal Prompts

29. How can you embrace imperfection in your life and the lives of others? How can you accept yourself daily?

Journal Prompts

30. What is one need of yours that you have been ignoring? It could be physical, emotional, or mental. How can you prioritize it today?

_____
_____
_____
_____
_____
_____
_____
_____
_____
_____
_____
_____
_____
_____
_____
_____
_____
_____
_____

MELISSA ALVIS